TO
EUROPE

S0-ABB-540

Mt. Hermon

Damascus

Tyre

Caesarea
Philippi

4

7

Ptolemais

Capernaum   Bethsaida

Cana   *SEA OF GALILEE*
Tiberias   *(or Lake Tiberias)*

Mt. Carmel

Nazareth

2

Caesarea

Mt. Tabor

6

TO THE
ORIENT
AND ASIA

JORDAN (River)

Sebasté
Samaria

Gerasa

Sychar

3

Mt. Gerizim

Joppa

Philadelphia

Arimathea

Jericho   5
Qumran (or Khirbet Qumran)

Jerusalem
Bethlehem

Ascalon

1

Machaerus

Gaza

Hebron

*DEAD
SEA*

Beersheba

Masada

8

TO AFRICA

0   6   12   18   24   30 miles

Experience Jesus Today

UNDERSTANDING
THE GOSPEL

Contemporary English Version

AMERICAN BIBLE SOCIETY
NEW YORK

PUBLISHER:
ABS - 1865 Broadway - New York, NY 10023-7505
Tel. (212) 408-1200

LAYOUT:
Studio Bayle

TEXT:
Edited by ABS

ILLUSTRATIONS:
Christian Heinrich - Natalie Louis-Lucas - Chantal Muller van den Berghe

PRINTING:
Graficas Estella - Estella - Spain

INTRODUCTION

*This book offers to help you
meet the Jesus of the Gospels.
This encounter is awe-inspiring:
it will change your life!
When someone meets Jesus Christ,
life, love, solidarity, sharing,
the struggle for justice, faith,
hope are all understood
in a radically new light.*

*This book hopes to awaken in you
a burning desire to search,
to contemplate, to listen
and to put into practice the Word
of the One who reveals God's
tenderness and offers it as a gift
to all the peoples of the earth.*

*This book plans to introduce you
to the joy of knowing Jesus the Son
and of living in his presence
a whole life offered in love
in his own image.*

*This book invites you
to an encounter.
Won't you accept?*

THIS BOOK IS DIVIDED INTO THREE PARTS:

- PART ONE:

History

This section provides the background to Jesus' life; it presents the beginnings of the gospels and shows how the gospel message remains Good News for today.

- PART TWO:

Good News

This section immerses us in the four gospels, examining the life of Jesus from his birth to the sending of the Holy Spirit. Each chapter highlights an important moment in Jesus' life. Thus, his words, his actions, his miracles, his parables, his Good News are laid out before our searching eyes. Each chapter, each "moment" of Jesus' life, is presented the same way:

- In Jesus' Time: the historical background

- In Gospel Times: how this event was understood in the early Church

- Reading: a passage from one of the four gospels or the Book of Acts, with questions to lead to deeper understanding of the event

- Living Today: how this event affects modern men and women

- Praying Today: how this event inspires prayer and action today.

- PART THREE:

Glossary

This section resembles a small dictionary. It presents, in alphabetical order, some of the words which appear frequently in the gospels or in the Bible in general. By clarifying the meaning of these words, this glossary gives the reader greater access to the riches of the biblical world.

I

History

IN JESUS' TIME

OUR WORLD
TWO THOUSAND YEARS AGO

It is believed that approximately 180 million people were living on earth at the time of Jesus' birth. Human beings had been in existence for many millennia. They had already developed many things: pottery, weaving, iron, the wheel, farming, raising animals, writing, painting, music, mathematics and even astronomy. But they hadn't yet imagined steam engines, electricity, trains, cars, planes, space stations, televisions or computers.

ACROSS THE CONTINENTS

At that time, North and South America were inhabited by different tribal peoples – from the Inuit in the North who hunted seals and caribou, to other tribes in the Amazon rain forest who grew a variety of grains. In North Africa, the Egyptian pyramids were already two thousand years old. The rest of the African continent was inhabited by different tribes, about whom little is known today. The few people living in Australia were hunters and gatherers. But in Asia, China was already a very powerful empire protected by a great wall over two hundred years old. Japan was inhabited by different groups of peoples who cultivated rice and made things from metal.

THE ROMAN EMPIRE

In the south of Europe, near the Mediterranean sea, the Roman army occupied many countries. These countries are known today as Italy, Spain, Portugal, France, Yugoslavia, Greece, Bulgaria, Turkey, Syria, Lebanon, Israel, Egypt, Libya, Tunisia, Algeria and Morocco. Beyond the borders of these countries lived people whom the Romans called "barbarians." A tribe of people called "Celts" lived in present day Great Britain and Ireland, and Teutons had come from Scandinavia to live in Germany. There were nomadic people on the steppes who wandered far and wide between Hungary and China.

RELIGION

All these women and men had some form of religious belief. Most of them were polytheists, which means that they believed in several different gods. They often considered natural happenings to be interventions by spirits or gods. Worship of these gods played an important role in society. Some of the major religions also existed at that time: Buddhism in India, Confucianism in China and Judaism in Palestine. The Jewish people had been waiting for a long time for God to send them a Savior.

"THE GOD WHO SAVES"

At this time, a Jewish couple from Palestine, Joseph and Mary, were traveling towards a southern town known as Bethlehem. It was in this little town that Mary gave birth to their first child, a boy whom they named Jesus. Jesus means "God saves," or "the God who saves." Jesus was the boy's first name. No one used last names, but rather, the first name of the child was followed by the first name of the father. For example, Jesus was called, "Jesus, son of Joseph."

A LITTLE VILLAGE

After Jesus was born, the family returned to Nazareth, a little village in the foothills, in the northern part of the country called Galilee. Jesus spent his childhood, his teenage years and a good part of his adult life there. The gospels don't tell us much about this period in Jesus' life, but it isn't difficult to piece together what his life was like.

LANGUAGE

Jesus lived like the other children around him. He learned to speak Aramaic with the accent typical of his area. Some of his first words were probably "immah" (mama) and "abbah" (dada). Later he learned Hebrew, the sacred language of the Jewish people. Aramaic and Hebrew are similar languages, a little bit like Arabic. Jesus must also have learned several Greek or Latin words used by soldiers, merchants and the Roman government.

EVERYDAY LIFE

In Nazareth, Jesus grew up knowing village life. He watched his mother go to the well for water, make bread with yeast, and season their food with spices. He saw Joseph work as a carpenter and carry large wooden beams. Jesus watched the shepherd leading the sheep, the farmer sowing seeds, the vine grower taking care of the vines. Jesus had friends. Together they played in the village square. Later, these same friends had difficulty believing that Jesus was any different from them. They would always see him as "the carpenter's son."

HOPE FOR THE POOR

Jesus also discovered suffering — beggars, the sick, lepers, orphans, the poor, slaves, prisoners, people who were abandoned. Jesus shared their hope of finding a better life. He heard them speak of revolutionaries who wanted to end the Roman occupation but who were sometimes put to death by the Roman soldiers.

All of this touched Jesus very deeply. The suffering he saw moved him more deeply than pictures that we see on television today and forget tomorrow. This poverty and sadness penetrated Jesus, shaping the way he viewed life, the people around him and his future.

A SON OF THE LAW

Jesus was Jewish. Like every Jewish boy, he was circumcised on the eighth day after he was born. His religious education initially took place in his family. On the Sabbath, Jesus went with Joseph to the synagogue where he learned all about the Jewish Law (the first books of the Bible). In school at the synagogue, he learned to recite prayers and the commandments and to read the Law in Hebrew. He would read passages from this book out loud in public. Like his father, he would cover himself with a "tallith" (a prayer shawl) and go to the house of prayer.

CELEBRATIONS

All year long, different celebrations served as reminders of the history and traditions shared by the Jewish people. Rosh Hashanah, or the "New Year," recalled the creation of the world. Passover brought to mind the liberation of the Israelites who were led out of Egypt by Moses. The "Harvest Festival" or Pentecost celebrated the gift of the covenant (a formal agreement) on Mount Sinai. The "Festival of Shelters" helped the people recall their long journey through the desert.

AT THE TEMPLE

When Jesus was twelve he went to Jerusalem with his parents. He saw so many new things: the bustling town, the splendid Temple, many other pilgrims from different countries, the throngs of merchants, the impressive presence of Roman soldiers, and scholars with whom he could discuss the Law. When he entered the Temple, Jesus also discovered how people were separated into different categories. There were special places for non-Jews, women, Israelite men, priests and the high priest.

THE CARPENTER

From the time he was twelve until the age of thirty, Jesus continued to live in Nazareth. He helped Joseph, the village carpenter, and probably replaced him. He worked with his hands to earn a living. During these years a feeling was growing in his heart. He was discovering more and more about himself and about God. No one else in the town, in his family or among his friends understood what was happening. One day he decided to take a big step and leave his village. He knew he had a message for all of humanity. Jesus went from his quiet village life to a life in the public eye. It was in the fifteenth year of the reign of the Roman emperor Caesar Tiberius, about 27 A.D.

AN UNUSUAL PERSON

Crowds from every corner of the country were coming to the Jordan River to see an unusual person. He dressed in camels' hair and ate food that he found in the desert: locusts and wild honey. He announced horrible events and warned everyone that they needed to convert — to change their hearts and the way they acted. As a sign that people wanted this change, he would immerse them in the waters of the Jordan River to baptize them. Their lives were completely changed. This man's name was John, but everyone referred to him as John the Baptist. He was Jesus' cousin and they were about the same age.

WHICH PATH TO TAKE?

Jesus left Nazareth for the Jordan River, where he was baptized by John. It was such a turning point in his life that he had to withdraw alone to the desert for time to pray. He thought about his future and about which path he should take. He was tempted by easy success, by ideas that could only come from the Evil One. Jesus chose the difficult path that would lead to his death on a cross. But this path gave all of humanity a new

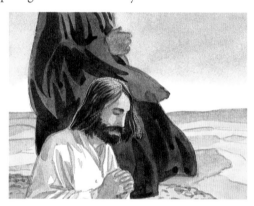

choice. When he came back from the desert, Jesus joined John in his ministry. But this lasted only a short time because King Herod Antipas had John locked up in a fortress on the other side of the Dead Sea. King Herod didn't appreciate what John was saying about his private life. He was even afraid that John's followers — his disciples — might start a rebellion.

A TEAM

John had prepared the way for Jesus. But Jesus wasn't alone; he liked to work as part of a team. But who would work with him? Jesus didn't ask priests from Jerusalem, or leaders, or scholars; instead he chose fishermen, craftspeople, a tax collector—ordinary folk. A group of women also joined them. This team traveled on foot throughout Galilee, through towns and villages and on the shores of the lake.

THE KINGDOM

Jesus' message was simple. He proclaimed the "coming of the Kingdom of God." These words don't mean a lot to us today. But for people in Jesus' time, it meant total change — no more misery, poverty, hunger or Roman domination. He proclaimed a time when justice, peace and happiness would reign. This very message of Jesus was heard as the Good News of God.

BE HEALED!

Many sick people came to find Jesus: the blind, the lame, the paralyzed, the deaf, the mute, lepers, the mentally ill. They were not only physically and emotionally hurt, they were often excluded from society and forced to beg for a living. People thought that God was punishing them or that they were possessed by an evil spirit. Healing for them was not only physical; it also meant that they would be accepted again by society and would feel loved — by themselves and by God.

To them, Jesus had the power to heal. There were many healers in those days when medicine was poorly developed. The sick begged for healing. Jesus laid his hands on them, asking them to believe in him, and they were healed. Jesus didn't use magic. He didn't ask for money. He shared the hopes and dreams of the sick. Jesus saw the healings as a sign of God's Kingdom.

SUSPICION

The apostles and disciples who followed Jesus were comfortable with many different kinds of people — the poor and the rich, craftspeople, farmers, tax collectors and Roman soldiers, as well as Jews, foreigners, women and men, adults and children. Such freedom annoyed the religious leaders.

For the religious leaders, there were on the one hand "good" people (the righteous) with whom they could associate, and on the other hand "bad" people (the unrighteous) with whom they couldn't associate. The chief priests sent "inspectors" to watch Jesus and to find fault with him — "You eat with tax collectors and sinners! You don't respect Moses' law! You don't fast according to the Law!" They were jealous of Jesus because he spoke the truth. He taught with authority. He didn't pay lip service to empty rules as they did.

WHO IS THIS JESUS?

Little by little people began to ask questions — "Who is Jesus? Where is he from? Is he a prophet? Is this the Messiah for whom we have been waiting, the one sent from God?" His enemies said he was possessed by the devil. Jesus didn't make any claims about who he was. He acted in keeping with the tradition of the prophets. He proclaimed the Good News. And he did it very well. He talked to God in a personal way as if to his father. Sometimes he spoke of a mysterious figure, the "Son of Man."

The people of his time were expecting a "Son of Man" who would come to judge humanity at the end of the world.

A GREAT CELEBRATION

Bigger and bigger crowds began to follow Jesus everywhere he went. He spoke to them. He healed them. He fed them. The gospels describe a gathering of thousands of people where everyone was fed because a few fish and a few loaves of bread were shared. It was a great celebration with much excitement. "We need a leader! Let's make Jesus king! He's better than Herod or Caesar!" A possible revolt was in the air. Jesus was aware of this, but refused it. His followers were disappointed and went home. Many companions now left him. They didn't understand the meaning of the shared bread.

IN FOREIGN COUNTRIES

The best thing for Jesus was to leave Galilee. With his small group of faithful followers, Jesus traveled into non-Jewish territory, on the other side of the Jordan River. This way he could avoid the people of Galilee who didn't understand him, the religious leaders who continued to spy on him and King Herod who wanted to kill him. By traveling abroad (he also went to Phoenicia and Samaria), Jesus wanted to show that he hadn't come for the sons and daughters of Israel alone but he had come for all humanity. Jesus took some time to reflect and talk with his friends before beginning the final phase of his life.

JERUSALEM

It was springtime. Throughout the Roman Empire and especially in Palestine, preparation was under way for the Jewish pilgrimage to Jerusalem at Passover. This great gathering celebrated the liberation of the Israelites from Egypt by Moses and his God. Jerusalem, the capital of a small Jewish state, numbered 25,000 inhabitants. Jerusalem's population doubled during such pilgrimages. This was also David's ancient royal city built in the time when Israel was a free nation. Jerusalem was the center of government where important officials were found — the high priest, the political and religious leader; Pontius Pilate, the governor sent by Rome with his soldiers to rule the city; the High Council, or Sanhedrin, a court made up of important priests, elders and scholars. All these officials were anxious about the upcoming Passover celebration. Above all, a rebellion against Rome had to be avoided.

CONFUSED AND AFRAID

This year Jesus decided to go to Jerusalem for Passover. It wasn't his first time there, but this time Jesus went publicly. Jesus knew what awaited him, and that he would be sentenced to death, but nonetheless he decided to go. A prophet must speak his message even in Jerusalem, at the risk of losing his life. Jesus' disciples followed him, confused and afraid.

ON A DONKEY

Friends from Galilee caught up with Jesus and his followers along the way. As he neared Jerusalem, Jesus got on a donkey. He wanted to show that he came to make peace. A warrior rode a horse; Jesus rode a donkey. Other friends were already in Jerusalem and came to meet him. The crowd grew bigger. It was a celebration! Cries of support rang out, "God bless the one who comes in the name of the Lord! God bless the coming Kingdom of our ancestor David!" Many thought that Jesus was the new David — a king who would liberate them from the Romans and who would establish Israel's freedom.

THE CUP OVERFLOWS

Jesus' last week began. He went to spend the night with some friends in Bethany, a village about two miles from Jerusalem. During the day Jesus went to the Temple with his disciples.

The space around the Temple had become a giant marketplace where animals were sold for sacrifice: bulls, sheep, goats and doves. The priests weren't bothered by this practice; in fact, they profited from it. Jesus got angry. He threw all the sellers out. The Temple was God's house, and not a den of thieves. The leaders reacted. Jesus had overstepped his bounds; he had questioned their authority and cut off a source of revenue. He had been annoying them for a long time. Now they had had enough. It was time to get rid of him.

THE FAREWELL MEAL

Jesus continued to teach in the Temple, no longer choosing his words carefully. He denounced their leaders' lack of justice. He demanded justice. During this time his enemies were plotting. How could they arrest Jesus quietly? How could they find him at night among the crowds of pilgrims? Judas, one of the twelve apostles and the traitor, said he would help them.

On Thursday night Jesus and his disciples met for their Passover meal. It was a solemn and reflective time. Jesus' gestures and words would remain burned into the memories of his friends, "This is my body, given for you. This is my blood, poured out for you."

TAKEN PRISONER

After the meal Jesus and his disciples went to the outskirts of town to spend the night praying in an olive grove.

Jesus understood that his hour had come. He accepted it. A group of soldiers, led by Judas, caught up with Jesus and the other disciples. Jesus was arrested, chained and dragged in front of a court that had been assembled hastily in the middle of the night. His friends fled. Peter was frightened and three times denied knowing Jesus. The Jewish High Council accused Jesus of wanting to destroy the Temple. They took Jesus before Pontius Pilate, the bungling, cowardly Roman governor. Pilate was afraid because he didn't want to look bad in front of Caesar. Pontius Pilate understood that Jesus was innocent, and he tried to save him. But his efforts were in vain. Finally, he gave Jesus over to the soldiers to be crucified. He washed his hands of any responsibility.

BETWEEN TWO CRIMINALS

Jesus had to carry his cross by himself. He was crucified between two robbers on a small hill before the gates of Jerusalem. The official words describing his crime were written and hung above him on the cross — Jesus of Nazareth, King of the Jews (abbreviated INRI). It was a terrible, humiliating agony — to be crucified in front of curious onlookers, cruel enemies and desperate friends.

Jesus died at three o'clock in the afternoon. It was the night before the Sabbath. His body had to be taken down from the cross quickly. The two robbers were still not dead so the soldiers killed them.

THE BURIAL

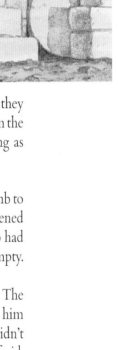

Joseph of Arimathea owned a garden near the place where Jesus was crucified. He offered to have Jesus' body placed in his tomb there. When Jesus' body was taken down from the cross it was placed hurriedly in the tomb carved out of rock. A large stone was rolled in front of the entrance. The Sabbath began.

The Sabbath day was normally a day of celebration. But for Jesus' friends it was a day of mourning. They felt like orphans — sad, abandoned, disappointed, hopeless and afraid. They didn't know whether the authorities were looking for them or not. All the hope they had in Jesus had died with him. The only thing left to do was to embalm the body of their master. Then they could go home and continue living as before.

THE EMPTY TOMB

The morning after the Sabbath some women went to the tomb to embalm the body. What they saw astonished and frightened them. The stone that had blocked the entrance to the tomb had been rolled away. Jesus' body was gone. The tomb was empty. What had happened?

Soon many accounts of people having seen Jesus emerged. The women, the disciples and friends of Jesus said they had seen him alive — in the garden, in a room, on the road and near the lake. They didn't recognize Jesus immediately. They hesitated. Sometimes they were afraid. Sometimes they weren't sure. But they eventually recognized him from a gesture (the sharing of bread), a word or a look. Their doubt was gone. They were sure. Jesus was alive. He had risen from the dead.

A NEW LIFE

Jesus wasn't alive like a dead person who has come back to life again. He didn't go back to living human life as before the cruci-fixion. He was transformed. "His body was put to death and his spirit was made alive" (1 Peter 3.18).

This unique experience of seeing him lasted only a short while. But it gave Jesus' friends the strength and the conviction to con-tinue what Jesus had begun. They received Jesus' Spirit, the Spirit of Pentecost. This would help them to go to the ends of the earth. A new page in history had begun; the story of the birth of the Church began.

WHEN THE GOSPELS WERE WRITTEN

Jesus wrote nothing during his lifetime. He was crucified in the year 30 A.D.
The gospels were written approximately between 65 and 95 A.D.
What happened during those years?

THE FIRST CHRISTIANS

Jesus' friends pulled themselves together. They didn't give up. With the strength of the Spirit, they proclaimed, "God had already planned and decided that Jesus would be handed over to you. So you took him and had evil men put him to death on a cross." The people who had killed Jesus weren't at all pleased. In the beginning Jesus' friends remained close to the Temple in Jerusalem. People considered them some sort of Jewish sect. Soon they were under suspicion and were persecuted. Stephen was stoned in 37 A.D.; he became the first Christian martyr. Most of Jesus' followers left Jerusalem to proclaim the Gospel in Samaria, Galilee and Syria. Antioch, the third-largest town in the Roman Empire, became an important center for them. This is where, for the first time, they were called "Christians," those who follow Christ.

CONVERSION OF THE PERSECUTOR

Paul was a zealous religious leader (a Pharisee). He was told by the priests in Jerusalem to find all the Christians and to put them in prison. On his way to Damascus, he came to understand, in a blinding flash, that persecuting Christians was the same as persecuting Jesus. This came as a great insight to him. Paul went to find the Christians and became one of them. He took time to reflect and pray. He became the most daring and outspoken of the disciples. For more than twenty years Paul traveled throughout the Roman Empire and founded communities in many towns. He visited them and wrote them letters (the Letters of Paul) to help them with their problems, their lives and their faith.

OPEN DOORS

Paul first addressed people in the "diaspora" or dispersal. This was the name given to the Jews (around four million) who were living outside of Palestine in towns under Roman rule. Soon many non-Jews became Christians. At that time there were two groups of Christians — those whose background was Judaism and those whose background was non-Jewish. The first group still observed Jewish law and used the Bible. The second group was vaguely familiar with Jewish tradition. People asked if becoming a Christian meant observing Jewish law as well. In the year 49 A.D., the disciples, who had gathered in Jerusalem, decided to open wide the doors to Christians who had come from a non-Jewish background. They decided that they didn't have to observe Jewish law.

THE BEGINNINGS OF ORGANIZATION

In the years following Jesus' death, Christians multiplied and began to get organized as communities. They often met together. They prayed together. They remembered Jesus' words and the things he had done. They repeated some of his gestures. They chose leaders: Deacons and elders joined the disciples. They shared everything they had. They proclaimed the Good News.

THE BELIEVERS REMEMBER

This Good News first spread by word of mouth. The disciples hadn't seen the need to write down Jesus' life and his teachings. Everyone remembered him. His friends had

very vivid memories of what he had done — how he had cured the sick, encountered sinners and the religious leaders; the many healings; the discussions with leaders; scandals in the Temple or when Jewish law wasn't respected; and the challenging parables he told. It was easy to tell about what they had seen and experienced. Nonetheless, many were still shocked by the humiliating death that Jesus had suffered. The disciples began to look for passages in the Jewish Scriptures that pointed to the fact that the long-awaited Messiah had to suffer and die on the cross.

THE FIRST WRITTEN RECORDS

Little by little the disciples began to write these stories down. They gathered collections of Jesus' words, his parables, stories of healing and discussions with the Pharisees. At first there were probably only scattered pieces in different groups and towns.

As time went on, those who knew Jesus were growing old. They were approaching death. New Christians wanted to know more and more about their Lord's life. It was time to think about writing everything down so that none of it would be lost. The political situation made this even more necessary. In Rome, in 64 A.D., the Christians were being persecuted by Nero. He accused them of setting fire to the city. From 66 to 70 A.D., a terrible war between Jewish revolutionaries and Romans ravaged Palestine. It ended with the destruction of the Temple in Jerusalem. The Temple was never rebuilt. From that date on Christianity would remain separate from Judaism. Christians were on their own.

FOUR VIEWS OF JESUS

The gospels are different from a day-to-day account of Jesus' life. They were probably written more than 30 years after his death. They were composed by four different authors at different times and places. The four versions of Jesus' life complement each other. They show us how Matthew, Mark, Luke and John understood Jesus' life in light of the resurrection. They knew that Jesus of Nazareth was the Messiah, the Christ, the Son of God, the Lord.

NEW PROBLEMS

But the evangelists didn't write only what they remembered. They didn't say only what they believed. They wrote for the Christians of their day. They tried, when telling about what Jesus did, to answer some of their questions — How should we pray? How can we interpret the Scriptures? What attitude should we take toward this Roman Emperor who thinks he is God? Should we still practice Jewish law? How can we spread the Good News? How can we help the poor? What is the greatest commandment? What about the future? How can we stay united when we are separated by so many miles? What should our attitude be toward the Pharisees? How can we choose our leaders?

MARK, FRIEND OF PETER

Mark was originally from Jerusalem. He was not one of the Twelve. He traveled first with Paul, then with Peter to proclaim the Good News. Peter was probably killed during Nero's persecution in 64 A.D. Mark may have begun to write his gospel because he wanted to preserve and pass on Peter's teachings.

It is believed that Mark was writing first and foremost for the Christians in Rome. Among them were Jews, Greeks, Romans, slaves and free people. Mark wrote in Greek and his language was simple, like that of Peter, the fisherman from the Lake of Galilee. Mark proclaimed "the good news about Jesus Christ, the Son of God" (Mark 1.1).

JESUS, SON OF GOD

Mark presented Jesus as someone who traveled around the countryside doing good deeds. He healed the sick, cast out demons, commanded nature and finally triumphed over death. As early as his baptism, and again at the transfiguration, God revealed that Jesus was his "own dear Son" (Mark 1.11; 9.7). Demons tried to reveal Jesus' identity (Mark 3.11; 5.7) but Jesus silenced them. It was only at his trial that Jesus allowed anyone to call him "the Son of the glorious God" (Mark 14.61, 62). In Mark's gospel, the only person who proclaimed his faith in the "Son of God" was the Roman soldier at the foot of the cross. By this Mark wanted to show that non-Jews were equally capable of recognizing who Jesus really was (Mark 15.39).

You will find passages from Mark's gospel in this book in chapters 5, 7, 8, 9, 10, 11, 16, 18, 19, 20, 21, 24, 25, 26, 27, 28, 32, 33 and 36.

LUKE, THE DOCTOR

Luke was born in Greece. He was a non-Jew who had become a Christian. He was also a physician. Luke was Paul's traveling companion. With Paul, Luke discovered the misery experienced by people living in the Mediterranean ports. Luke was writing particularly for those without hope – to the poor, women and slaves. He had never met Jesus but he was careful to ask many questions of those witnesses who were still alive, including Mary, Jesus' mother. His gospel is followed by another book, the Acts of the Apostles, that tells of the birth of the church. Luke wrote perhaps in the 70's or the 80's A.D. He was writing to Christians living in non-Jewish territory. He wrote his text very eloquently, in Greek.

JESUS, GOD'S GOODNESS

Luke began with a wonderful story of Jesus' birth. He then presented a Jesus who was full of goodness. Luke's Jesus was sometimes hard on the rich but welcomed the "little ones" – the poor, the unhappy, women and strangers. Luke shows Jesus as a friend of ordinary folk because "he came to look for and to save people who are lost" (Luke 19.10). Jesus told of God's goodness toward all humanity.

You will find passages from Luke in this book in chapters 1, 2, 4, 6, 22 and 35.

Also, you can look in your Bible for passages that show how Jesus reached out to the poor and sinners — his raising from death the only son of the widow of Nain (Luke 7.11-17); Jesus' unexpected visit to Zacchaeus, the unpopular tax collector (Luke 19.1-10); the parable of the proud Pharisee and the forgiven tax collector (Luke 18.9-14).

MATTHEW, THE TAX COLLECTOR

Matthew, or Levi, was originally from Palestine. He was a tax collector before he became a disciple. Matthew knew Jesus personally. His gospel was written in Greek perhaps between 65 and 80 A.D., or even later. Matthew was writing for Christians of Jewish background who were living in the Syria-Palestine area. These communities had a tendency to close in on themselves. It was important to keep them open to Christians with different backgrounds.

JESUS, SON OF DAVID

Matthew wrote for an audience who knew the history of the people of Israel. He presented Jesus as being deeply rooted in this history. Matthew's gospel begins with the family tree of Jesus Christ, who "came from the family of King David and also from the family of Abraham" (Matthew 1.1). He "is called the Messiah" (Matthew 1.16), the Messiah of the true Israel. He came to accomplish what the prophets had announced. He is also the Son of Man who will return at the end of time to judge all people according to what they have done.

You will find passages from Matthew in this book in chapters 3, 12, 13, 14, 17, 29, 30 and 31. Also, you can look in your Bible for passages that show how Matthew described the Pharisees. The Pharisees' opposition to Jesus didn't stop with his death; although some became Christians, many went on to persecute the early Christian communities (Matthew 23.1-36).

JOHN, A MAN OF REFLECTION

John was the youngest of the apostles, the "one that Jesus loved." He came from a family of fishermen from the lake in Galilee. His gospel is very different from the first three. He may have written it in the 90's A.D. in a Greek community, probably in Asia Minor (modern Turkey).

John's gospel is characterized by two things — on one hand, his writing is the result of much reflection. His thoughts are sometimes abstract — he talks a lot about love, light and truth. On the other hand, he has very specific memories of life in Jesus' time: place names, dates, buildings, the dispute between Jews and Samaritans, burial customs and purification rites.

JESUS, WORD OF GOD

John presented Jesus as the eternal Word who came from God into the world (John 1.9). Jesus came so that all might live a full life. Many of the things Jesus did were signs. The water that Jesus changed into wine at the wedding at Cana represented God's new covenant with humanity. The multiplication of bread announced the gift of Jesus himself to humanity. The healing of the man who was born blind illustrated that Jesus was the light of the world. The resurrection of Lazarus showed that Jesus was master of life.

You will find passages from John in this book in chapters 15, 34 and 38. You can also look up some other passages from John: the introductory hymn (John 1.1-18), the miracle at Cana (John 2.1-11), the healing of the man who was born blind (John 9.1-41), the raising of Lazarus (John 10.1-21), the parable of the vine (John 15.1-17) and the washing of the disciples' feet (John 13).

John reminds us strongly that Jesus calls us "to love each other" as he has loved us. "The greatest way to show love for friends is to die for them" (John 15.12-13).

The fourth gospel concludes in a way that holds true for the three other gospels (and even for this book) — "Jesus worked many other miracles for his disciples, and not all of them are written in this book. But these are written so that you will put your faith in Jesus as the Messiah and the Son of God. If you have faith in him, you will have true life" (John 20.30, 31).

LIVING AND PRAYING TODAY

The Gospels were written in Greek during the first century A.D. They are presented here in an English translation, the Contemporary English Version (CEV). These texts have lasted for 19 centuries. They do not contain easy clichés unrelated to today's life. These passages are filled with light and wisdom that continue to guide children, women and men in ever-changing situations.

We read these texts today, on the dawn of the third millennium.
We read them at an extraordinary time in human history:
- never before have there been so many scholars...
- never before has technology been so developed...
- never before have there been weapons capable of destroying the entire earth...
- never before has it been so easy to travel to different countries...
- never before have we been able to receive news from around the world so quickly...
- never before have human beings understood so clearly that we are all responsible for this planet...
- never before have so many people lived in poverty and died of hunger...
- never before has there been so much contact between people from different cultures and beliefs...
- never before has humankind had so much hope in the future...
- never before has the future been so feared...
- never before have we been so free to open or close our hearts to God in our Western culture...
- never before has the participation of the individual been so necessary in order to build a new world... as today.

We are reading these gospels today. Each time we read them we discover something new. Jesus' Spirit isn't dead. This Spirit can help us discover in a new way what the Gospel means for us today. The sections of this book entitled "LIVING TODAY" help us with this discovery.

II

The Good
News

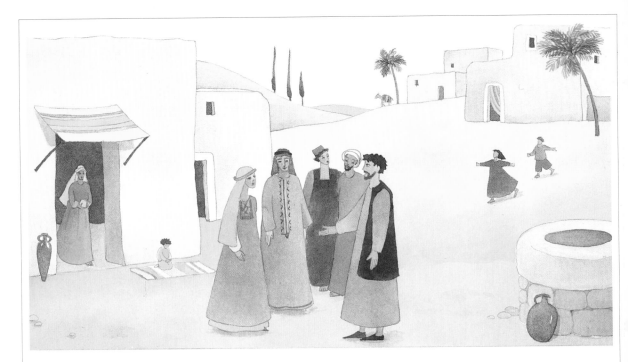

CHAPTER 1

THE ANNUNCIATION

IN JESUS' DAY

Mary, the woman who was to become Jesus' mother, was born in Nazareth, a small town of about 150 inhabitants. Nazareth was at the foot of the hills in Galilee, far from Jerusalem. Nazarenes weren't well liked by people in the neighboring villages. Sometimes they would say, "What good can come out of Nazareth?"

Like most twelve- to fifteen-year-old girls of her time, Mary had been promised in marriage. Traditionally, during the year following the official engagement, the young woman continued to live with her parents.

WHEN THE GOSPELS WERE WRITTEN

Luke wrote his account at least seventy years after the Annunciation. Imagine trying to tell someone about something that happened during the First World War in a town far from your home! But Luke was acquainted with Mary. He understood that she had offered her whole life to God, that she was "a servant of the Lord."

Around 70 to 80 A.D., Luke was among those Christians who saw Jesus, Mary's son, not only as an extraordinary man, but also as the Son of God.

Luke wanted to show that at the beginning of Jesus' life, both Mary and God were present. In Luke's day, when authors wanted to write about a person's life, they created a picture with words in the same way that a painter would paint a picture — in this case, the annunciation. From the very beginning, Luke insists on a particular message in his gospel. He offers the reader a clue — "The one we will speak about is not only a man. We recognize that he is also the Son of God!"

THE GOSPEL

²⁶ God sent the angel Gabriel to the town of Nazareth in Galilee ²⁷ with a message for a virgin named Mary. She was engaged to Joseph from the family of King David. ²⁸ The angel greeted Mary and said, "You are truly blessed! The Lord is with you."

²⁹ Mary was confused by the angel's words and wondered what they meant. ³⁰ Then the angel told Mary, "Don't be afraid! God is pleased with you, ³¹ and you will have a son. His name will be Jesus. ³² He will be great and will be called the Son of God Most High. The Lord God will make him king, as his ancestor David was. ³³ He will rule the people of Israel forever, and his kingdom will never end."

³⁴ Mary asked the angel, "How can this happen? I am not married!"

³⁵ The angel answered, "The Holy Spirit will come down to you, and God's power will come over you. So your child will be called the holy Son of God. ³⁶ Your relative Elizabeth is also going to have a son, even though she is old. No one thought she could ever have a baby, but in three months she will have a son. ³⁷ Nothing is impossible for God!"

³⁸ Mary said, "I am the Lord's servant! Let it happen as you have said." And the angel left her.

Luke 1.26-38

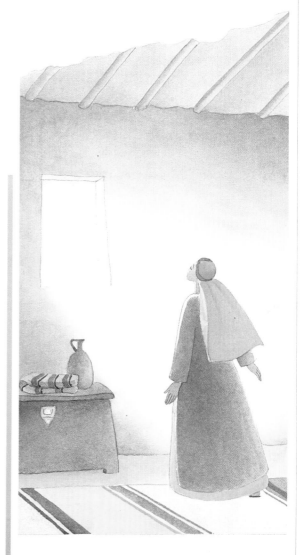

UNDERSTANDING THE TEXT

1. Look for titles given to the child who will be born, as well as his qualities and what he will do.

2. Look up the following words in the glossary: *angel, Gabriel, David, Jacob* and *Holy Spirit.*

3. Look for Galilee and Nazareth on the map.

THE DAY I WAS BORN

There was a time when I didn't exist. Now I exist because my parents' love brought me into the world. From the very moment my parents expected my birth, God looked on me with tenderness. What joy — the love of God is with me forever! God's love is as boundless and tender as the love of a mother and father for their child.

MY FAMILY NAME

My parents gave me a "family name," the one that they received from their parents. To be given a name is to be welcomed into a family; it is to belong. Others before me had this same name. I am now a part of a long tradition.

MY FIRST NAME

At the same time, my parents gave me a name that is just for me — my "first name." This "first name" makes me special among those who have the same "family name" as I. Those who know and love me call me by my first name. My first name is me!

GOD'S FAMILY

Christians are people who become God's children. They are baptized with the sign of water and the words "I baptize you in the name of the Father, and of the Son, and of the Holy Spirit." Through baptism they join the family of the Church, those who bear the name of the Son of God — Christ, from whom the name "Christian" comes.

A SIGN

*Lord of the annunciation,
you give a sign to the weak
and to the strong, to the humble
and to the powerful,
to all living creatures!*

*You call them by name,
as cherished children;
you tell them,
"With all my love,
I will always
be with you!"*

*Lord of the annunciation,
you give a sign to people
from every town and village,
from every neighborhood
and of all ages!
You call us by name
to be your messengers.
You trust us enough to ask,
"Will you carry my happiness
to all the children of the earth?"*

*Here we are, Lord, ready to work
with you to make marvelous
things happen in our world!*

CHAPTER 2
JESUS' BIRTH

IN JESUS' DAY

WHEN THE GOSPELS WERE WRITTEN

Bethlehem was a well-known city. There, one thousand years before, King David was born. During David's time, the Israelites were a free people. But in Jesus' day the country was occupied by Romans. In order to control the way taxes were collected, the Emperor of Rome, Caesar Augustus (who ruled from 27 B.C. to 14 A.D.) organized a census of the whole population.

Mary and Joseph traveled to Bethlehem to register for the census. They weren't able to find a place to stay because all the inns were full. Perhaps they would find someplace warm and dry to sleep — a cave or a stable. Jesus was born in that stable. His first cradle was a manger, where the animals ate.

When a child is born, we often take pictures. These pictures allow us to remember the baby's first look, first smile and first steps. In Jesus' day there were no photographs, no written records and not even birth certificates to record the precise place and date of birth.

So, many decades later, when Luke wanted to tell about the events surrounding Jesus' birth, he had no written documents to help him. Instead he relied on Mary's memories of the birth. Thanks to these memories, he was able to write a marvelous account, filled with angels, light, song and glory.

He didn't retell the birth of the newborn child in great detail. Instead, Luke wanted us to enter into the great story of Jesus' life.

To those who were expecting the Messiah to lead the fight against the Romans, Luke showed a God who brought peace. To those who believed in a far off, terrible God, Luke showed a God who became a small child. To those who thought that God spoke first to kings, to the powerful and the rich, Luke revealed a God who preferred those who were scorned — the shepherds in the countryside around Bethlehem.

THE GOSPEL

¹ About that time Emperor Augustus gave orders for the names of all the people to be listed in record books. ² These first records were made when Quirinius was governor of Syria.

³ Everyone had to go to their own hometown to be listed. ⁴ So Joseph had to leave Nazareth in Galilee and go to Bethlehem in Judea. Long ago Bethlehem had been King David's hometown, and Joseph went there because he was from David's family.

⁵ Mary was engaged to Joseph and traveled with him to Bethlehem. She was soon going to have a baby, ⁶ and while they were there, ⁷ she gave birth to her first-born son. She dressed him in baby clothes and laid him on a bed of hay, because there was no room for them in the inn.

[8] That night in the fields near Bethlehem some shepherds were guarding their sheep. [9] All at once an angel came down to them from the Lord, and the brightness of the Lord's glory flashed around them. The shepherds were frightened. [10] But the angel said, "Don't be afraid! I have good news for you, which will make everyone happy. [11] This very day in King David's hometown a Savior was born for you. He is Christ the Lord. [12] You will know who he is, because you will find him dressed in baby clothes and lying on a bed of hay."

[13] Suddenly many other angels came down from heaven and joined in praising God. They said:

[14] "Praise God in heaven!
Peace on earth to everyone
who pleases God."

Luke 2.1-14

UNDERSTANDING THE TEXT

1. Look for the new titles that are given to Jesus in this passage.

2. Look up the meaning of these titles in the glossary.

3. What is the angel's role in Luke's account?

4. Look for a sentence or phrase that could be used as a title for the passage.

5. Find Bethlehem on the map. What is the approximate distance from Nazareth to Bethlehem?

LIVING
TODAY

SHEPHERDS AND LITTLE PEOPLE

Shepherds have traditionally been "little" people! Being "little" does not refer to size! Being "little" also means lacking in importance. "Little" people don't get the same respect as everyone else — no one listens to them. They aren't allowed the same happiness as others. No one wants to be "little" in this way. People are forced into "littleness" by neglect, egoism and the scorn of others. God, as a loving parent, wants us all to be equal.

THE MANY

There are many "little" people — they don't have food, homes, or jobs. They don't have anything. They are shunned and ignored. "Little" people, like everyone else, have hearts full of love; they long to be "great" like everyone else! God is on the side of these "little" people. God wants to love and give attention to those who have nothing and to those who lack love and attention. God came to earth — born to live among those who are alone and are abandoned.

A GREAT JOY

The "little" ones were waiting for God. They needed love so much that their hearts and minds were wide open to welcome this Good News — God came to earth as a child! Jesus was born, "little" among the "little!" All of humanity was created to be great — in God's image — to belong and to be loved! What a great blessing!

THE CRADLE

*Friends,
look with your eyes:
there, in the cradle, this newborn.
This is our God!*

*Here is the one we were expecting!
God has come, after all,
to free us from the chains
that bind us, from evil
and the Evil One, from cruelty
that bares its claws,
from pride that fills its belly!
God has come, after all,
to save us! Jesus is born,
sent by God. Jesus has come
to change our hearts!*

*Friends,
look with all your love:
there, in the cradle, this newborn.
It is Jesus, our brother!
Here is the one we were expecting!
God has come, finally, to announce
that all people everywhere
are equal, that all the different
colored skins are the rainbow
of God's great love!
God has come to teach us
about peace and sharing!
God has come, finally, to save us!*

*It is he, Jesus Christ,
our God and brother!
Jesus has come to change the world!*

CHAPTER 3

THE WISE MEN

IN JESUS' DAY

Herod had been King of Judea for more than thirty years when Jesus was born. He was a foreigner who became king thanks to the support of the Romans. He was detested. He forced his decisions on everyone. His "police" were everywhere. He was becoming more and more afraid of losing his throne. Five days before his death, Herod even had one of his sons executed! Matthew's gospel tells of the massacre of innocent children, ordered by Herod, shortly after Jesus' birth (Matthew 2.16-18).

WHEN THE GOSPELS WERE WRITTEN

Herod had been dead for many decades when Matthew wrote his gospel. But Herod was not forgotten. Matthew was writing to Christians who had converted from Judaism. They were called "Judeo-Christians."

At first they met among themselves. But, little by little, people from other religions and countries joined their group — non-Jews and foreigners. Matthew showed them that even as early as Jesus' birth, foreigners — wise men from the east — were led to Jesus. Faith in Jesus Christ was open to all people.

There was a Jewish tradition that the day foreigners came to Jerusalem bearing gifts a new era would begin. And according to the gospel, the wise men brought gifts to Jesus — a new page in the history of humanity had been turned!

The first Christians were often persecuted. In recalling the figure of the bloodthirsty Herod, Matthew shows that persecution was a part of Jesus' life and that of the early Christians from the very beginning.

THE GOSPEL

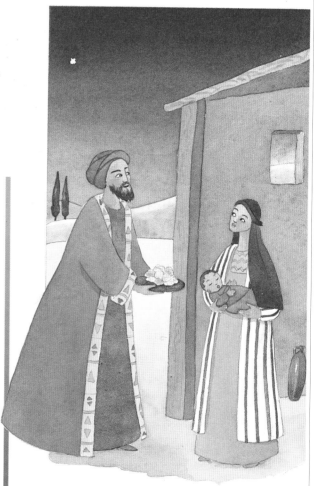

[1] When Jesus was born in the village of Bethlehem in Judea, Herod was king. During this time some wise men from the east came to Jerusalem [2] and said, "Where is the child born to be king of the Jews? We saw his star in the east and have come to worship him."

[3] When King Herod heard about this, he was worried, and so was everyone else in Jerusalem. [4] Herod brought together the chief priests and the teachers of the Law of Moses and asked them, "Where will the Messiah be born?"

[5] They told him, "He will be born in Bethlehem, just as the prophet wrote:

[6] 'Bethlehem in the land
of Judea,
you are very important
among the towns of Judea.
From your town
will come a leader,
who will be like a shepherd
for my people Israel.'"

[7] Herod secretly called in the wise men and asked them when they had first seen the star. [8] He told them, "Go to Bethlehem and search carefully for the child. As soon as you find him, let me know. I want to go and worship him too." [9] The wise men listened to what the king said and then left. And the star they had seen in the east went on ahead of them until it stopped over the place where the child was. [10] They were thrilled and excited to see the star.

[11] When the men went into the house and saw the child with Mary, his mother, they knelt down and worshiped him. They took out their gifts of gold, frankincense, and myrrh and gave them to him. [12] Later they were warned in a dream not to return to Herod, and they went back home by another road.

Matthew 2.1–12

UNDERSTANDING THE TEXT

1. Try to find on the map the route that the wise men took.

2. What is the star's function in this passage? Compare this with the angel's role in Luke's story, page 31.

3. What expression shows that Herod is afraid of losing his throne?

4. What are the new titles given to Jesus in this passage?

5. Look up the meaning of the following words in the glossary: *wise men (Magi), gold, frankincense and myrrh.*

Seekers

To find God you must search — with all your heart and all your mind. Christians are people who search for God! Like the wise men, they are alert. With their love and intelligence they are on the lookout for signs of God's presence. They are not proud, thinking that they know everything about God! They are constantly attentive. Their faith leads them to discover signs of God.

Signs

As God did for the wise men, God places "stars" on the road we walk. These signs show us that God is nearby. There are many of these signs that draw our eyes to God — people who help and console each other and who try to make the world more beautiful in God's image, people who pray and sing about their faith in God, people who hear the Gospel as Good News, people who get together in Jesus' name and act according to God's love, and people who see world events as a call to work. There are "stars" for everyone on our journey toward God.

Foreigners

The wise men were foreigners because they traveled from a different land! In God's eyes there are no foreigners to be pushed aside or rejected because of their race, country, religion, clothes, poverty or wealth. For God, there are only human beings to whom joy is offered! The whole world needs to know the happiness of being loved by God! That is why God's Son, Jesus, was born among us.

Differences

Everyone is different. Fortunately! Each of the wise men came with a different gift. Because of these differences — in personality and origin — each of us is able to bring something unique and beautiful. What a splendid treasure it makes when everything is put together!

STARS

Lord, you tell me:

"Give everyone
the right to food and to respect,
and you will be a star
of generosity!

Bridge the gaps
of hate and jealousy
that separate human beings
and you will be a star
of forgiveness!

Announce that every living
creature, regardless
of nationality, sin, levèl
of intelligence, job or religion,
is called to be
God's precious child,
and you will be
a star of welcome!"

Make us stars, Lord,
shining stars in the darkness
of the world, so that we may find
your loving smile giving light
to all our world!

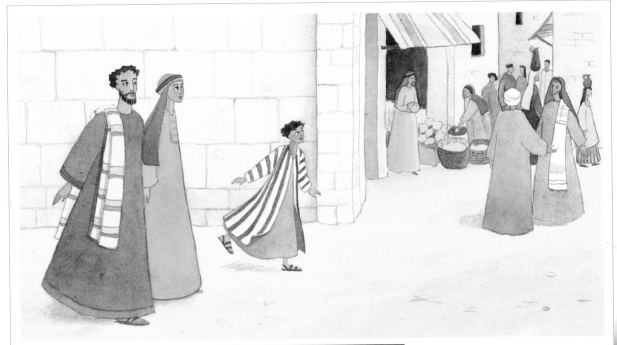

CHAPTER 4

WHEN JESUS WAS TWELVE

IN JESUS' DAY

A trip to Jerusalem was an extraordinary adventure for a young boy from the country. Jesus made this trip when he was twelve years old. His parents took him on a pilgrimage to "the holy city." Everything was new – the trip through the countryside, that took several days, new friends, the square before the Temple, the week-long celebrations.

Near the Temple, famous instructors were teaching, asking and answering questions put forward by young and old pilgrims. Jesus joined a group and participated in the discussion. He was so caught up in everything that he didn't return to his parents.

WHEN THE GOSPELS WERE WRITTEN

Jesus lived in Nazareth for thirty years. The gospels only mention one event during this whole time – the pilgrimage to Jerusalem. Why did Luke think it would be useful to tell this story? When he wrote this passage the Temple in Jerusalem may have already been destroyed by the Roman troops (in the year 70 A.D.). It was never rebuilt. But scholars familiar with the Law continued to teach anyway. They even founded a school in Jamnia, in the region of Galilee. Perhaps Luke wanted to show Christians that, from the beginning, Jesus' teaching was more astonishing than that of the scholars.

In this passage, Luke has Jesus speak for the first time. Whom does Jesus talk about but "my Father"! Jesus reveals a new way of seeing God – a God who is his Father, and of whom Jesus is the Son.

This is not easy to understand. Luke shows his readers that they are not the only ones to find it difficult. Even Jesus' parents "did not understand what he meant."

THE GOSPEL

⁴¹ Every year Jesus' parents went to Jerusalem for Passover. ⁴² And when Jesus was twelve years old, they all went there as usual for the celebration. ⁴³ After Passover his parents left, but they did not know that Jesus had stayed on in the city. ⁴⁴ They thought he was traveling with some other people, and they went a whole day before they started looking for him. ⁴⁵ When they could not find him with their relatives and friends, they went back to Jerusalem and started looking for him there.

⁴⁶ Three days later they found Jesus sitting in the temple, listening to the teachers and asking them questions. ⁴⁷ Everyone who heard him was surprised at how much he knew and at the answers he gave.

⁴⁸ When his parents found him, they were amazed. His mother said, "Son, why have you done this to us? Your father and I have been very worried, and we have been searching for you!"

⁴⁹ Jesus answered, "Why did you have to look for me? Didn't you know that I would be in my Father's house?" ⁵⁰ But they did not understand what he meant.

⁵¹ Jesus went back to Nazareth with his parents and obeyed them. His mother kept on thinking about all that had happened.

⁵² Jesus became wise, and he grew strong. God was pleased with him and so were the people.

Luke 2.41-52

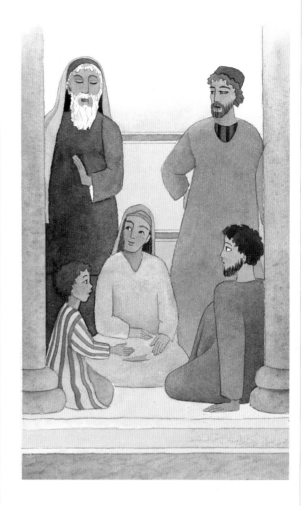

UNDERSTANDING THE TEXT

1. The word *father* is used twice in this passage. What are the meanings of both uses of the word?

2. With what people and what groups does Jesus associate?

3. Look up the meaning of the following words in the glossary: *Passover, Temple, scribe* and *revelation*.

TWELVE YEARS OLD

Often at the age of twelve we decide that childhood is too limited. We have to get away from it, quickly! There is so much to discover and it is so exciting to begin searching alone, without always being supervised by someone! We think that older people haven't thought of everything, and that there are so many things left to discover. Perhaps we can do better than our elders? So we think, we search, we want to understand, we talk and we argue. There is something that needs to be said, and we want to be heard, to be taken into consideration! Why should our elders be the only ones who are right?

A CHILD LISTENS AND SPEAK

As a child about to become a young man, Jesus joined in the adults' intellectual discussions about God. He had learned a lot from Joseph his father and the leaders of the synagogue; he needed to hear so much more, to know more; he had many questions to ask and now he had the opportunity to be in his "Father's house." Between God in heaven and Jesus there is the same special bond as between a parent and a child. This was hard for the masters in the Temple and for his parents to understand! Perhaps it takes a child's heart to talk about God and to realize how much God is a loving parent.

GROWING

In wisdom: our minds and hearts become more and more open to the gospel. We become better able to choose the only treasure, the only jewel that is worth anything — the ability to love like Jesus Christ!

In size: we let go of what is "little," of our old habits. We put our minds and bodies to work to transform the world in Jesus Christ's way.

God and others are pleased with us: we practice Jesus' gospel and live like children of God. Then we see God's beauty and love appear in our words and actions.

YOUTH

*Loving God, I am young!
I don't know every language.
I don't possess great knowledge.
I don't know the whole Bible.
I am not a scholar.
But I believe with all my heart
and with all my mind
that Jesus is your Son,
the Lord whom I love!*

*I know him!
Jesus was young,
like me!
He talked, he played,
he looked for answers,
like me!
Jesus laughed, he ran,
he cried, he was comforted,
like me!
He learned to read,
he learned to choose,
he learned to make decisions,
like me!*

*What joy —
the Lord Jesus was young
like me!
Through Jesus I want to learn
to love God
and my neighbors.
With Jesus, I want to grow!*

JESUS' BAPTISM

IN JESUS' DAY

John the Baptist was Jesus' older cousin by a few months. John didn't become a priest like his father, Zechariah. But he had spent some time in the desert, perhaps with the Jewish monks of Qumran. (The Qumran library was discovered in 1947 in a series of caves near the Dead Sea.) With the monks John would have learned about their frugal life and about purification by water.

John the Baptist preached a simple lifestyle. He also preached about a baptism for the forgiveness of sins. He was very well known and respected. He would immerse people in the Jordan River to baptize them. ("To baptize" means "to immerse".) When they came out they were considered pure and made the decision to live a new life. The "baptized" lived a total transformation — a conversion.

When Jesus heard about what John was doing, he decided to leave Nazareth to join him. Jesus asked John to baptize him. But John felt that Jesus would soon go further than he had ever gone.

Before continuing, Jesus went to the desert to take some time to meditate and pray. He thought about the path his life would take. It would not be an easy path.

Not long after, John the Baptist was arrested by Herod. Jesus then began to proclaim the Good News himself. John the Baptist had prepared the way for Jesus.

WHEN THE GOSPELS WERE WRITTEN

The beginning verses of Mark's gospel are found on the following page. They were written about sixty to seventy years after Jesus' birth. The gospel isn't just a book; it announces the Good News of Jesus Christ, Son of God.

Mark wanted his readers to see that this beginning wasn't the beginning of just any story. That is why he surrounded Jesus' baptism with astonishing signs, seen by Jesus alone — the skies were torn open and the Holy Spirit descended like a dove. The voice of God introduced his son, Jesus.

Mark also made the point that Jesus had to struggle to find his way. This is the meaning of the forty days in the desert where Jesus was encouraged by the Holy Spirit, tempted by Satan, served by angels, and accompanied by wild animals.

JESUS' BAPTISM

THE GOSPEL

¹ This is the good news about Jesus Christ, the Son of God. ² It began just as God had said in the book written by Isaiah the prophet,

"I am sending my messenger
to get the way ready
for you.
³ In the desert
someone is shouting,
'Get the road ready
for the Lord!
Make a straight path
for him.'"

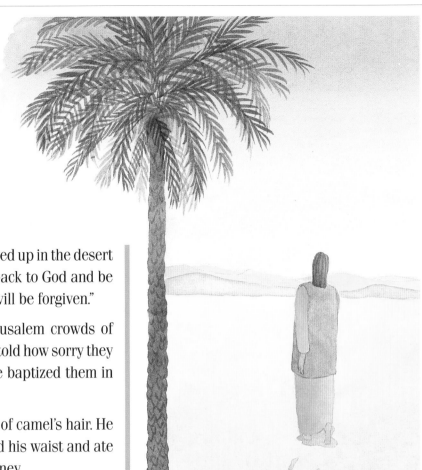

⁴ So John the Baptist showed up in the desert and told everyone, "Turn back to God and be baptized! Then your sins will be forgiven."

⁵ From all Judea and Jerusalem crowds of people went to John. They told how sorry they were for their sins, and he baptized them in the Jordan River.

⁶ John wore clothes made of camel's hair. He had a leather strap around his waist and ate grasshoppers and wild honey.

⁷ John also told the people, "Someone more powerful is going to come. And I am not good enough even to stoop down and untie his sandals. ⁸ I baptize you with water, but he will baptize you with the Holy Spirit!"

⁹ About that time Jesus came from Nazareth in Galilee, and John baptized him in the Jordan River. ¹⁰ As soon as Jesus came out of the water, he saw the sky open and the Holy Spirit coming down to him like a dove. ¹¹ A voice from heaven said, "You are my own dear Son, and I am pleased with you."

¹² Right away God's Spirit made Jesus go into the desert. ¹³ He stayed there for forty days while Satan tested him. Jesus was with the wild animals, but angels took care of him.

Mark 1.1-13

UNDERSTANDING THE TEXT

1. What title did Mark give to his gospel?

2. How did the voice from heaven introduce Jesus?

3. Look up the meanings of the following words in the glossary: *gospel, Isaiah, John the Baptist, baptism, dove, Satan* and *forty*.

4. Look for the following places on the map: the Jordan River where John baptized; Judea and Jerusalem, from where many people came to see John; Nazareth, Jesus' home; the desert where Jesus went to pray.

LIVING TODAY

THE BEGINNING

Certain events can change your entire life — for example, meeting someone, starting a new job, a tragedy, a great joy, a call that you feel in your heart and mind to help others, or the realization that you are loved by God. After these experiences, you look at the world differently and act differently. These events are like a new birth.

THE GOSPEL

Jesus Christ is the gospel, or the Good News of God for the world. Through Jesus, God speaks the Word that brings us to life. With Jesus, women and men see the tender face of God who is in heaven. This gospel, this Good News, this Jesus Christ, calls us to begin a new life!

THE DESERT

Sometimes it is difficult to keep following the path we have chosen, to keep walking the road we set out on at our baptism. So many other roads rise up before us and seem so appealing. At these times it is important to look deep inside ourselves. We need to step aside, like going into the desert — to think, to pray and to let Jesus Christ light the way. Then we are again free to choose the way of the gospel.

CONVERSION

When we decide to follow Jesus' way, God accepts us as a child and tells us, "I am giving you all my love. Do you want to give me your love, as a beloved child, and walk with me and my other beloved children?" Sometimes we stray from God's path — we don't listen to God any more, we don't pray, we ignore truth and goodness, we allow evil to dwell in us, we forget, we turn away. Conversion is a turning back toward God to say, "Please forgive me, I've made a mistake! I have sinned against you. But love and joy are found in the Gospel! Life is greater with you! I'm coming back!"

JESUS IS THE ONE

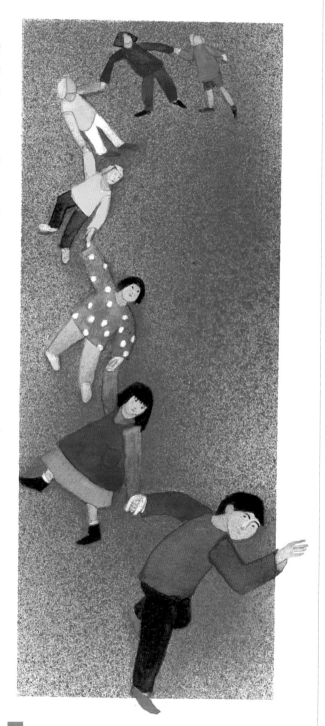

Jesus!
It is he!
He's coming!
Jesus is among us,
with us,
as one of us!

Jesus is the one who proclaims
that all his friends
are God's delight.
Jesus is the one who frees
prisoners from evil and fear.
Jesus is the one who guides
us along the path to become
children of God, and brothers
and sisters to all living creatures.
Jesus is the one who offers
his cross to the world
as a sign of love
and as the rising sun.
Jesus is the one who speaks
of God and tells us
that God is a loving parent.
Jesus is the best thing
that ever happened to the world!

Our minds are made up —
we will walk with Jesus,
and with Jesus, discover life.

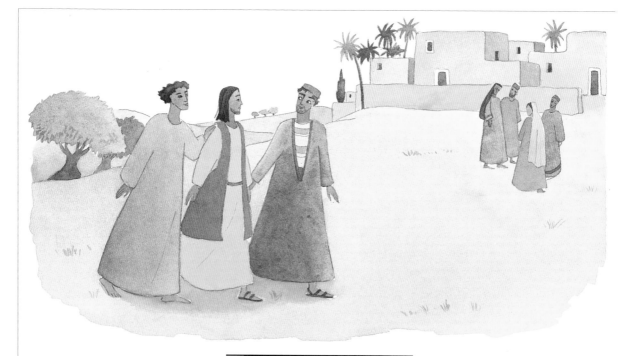

CHAPTER 6

JESUS IN NAZARETH

IN JESUS' DAY

Jesus lived in Nazareth for thirty years. When he left his village, his friends and family were amazed, "Why doesn't the carpenter stay with us? He knows everyone. There is plenty of work in the village!" Soon, they would hear of the things Jesus was doing in the region — he was proclaiming an extraordinary message, the sick were being healed and crowds were following him.

One day, Jesus came back to Nazareth, his hometown. His neighbors didn't know what to think — some admired him while others criticized him. Some even wanted him to go away and wanted to hurt him.

WHEN THE GOSPELS WERE WRITTEN

When Luke tells of Jesus' public life, he places the return to Nazareth at the very beginning of his gospel. Luke shows us Jesus explaining his mission before the entire synagogue. This mission had already been written in a book in the Hebrew Bible (Hebrew Scriptures). But now it was becoming a reality.

When he wrote his text, Luke thought about all Jesus had done for the poor, the sick, prisoners and the oppressed. But he also thought about all the suffering that he, Luke, had seen. He was a doctor and met a lot of sick people. He traveled to Rome with Paul. He saw beggars by the road, slaves working at the docks, prisoners on boats and behind bars.

When he wrote this passage, Luke also thought about all those people to whom he had proclaimed Jesus' message of freedom. Like Jesus' neighbors in Nazareth, not everyone welcomed Luke's message.

¹⁶ Jesus went back to Nazareth, where he had been brought up, and as usual he went to the meeting place on the Sabbath. When he stood up to read from the Scriptures, ¹⁷ he was given the book of Isaiah the prophet. He opened it and read,

> ¹⁸ The Lord's Spirit
>   has come to me,
> because he has chosen me
> to tell the good news
>   to the poor.
> The Lord has sent me
> to announce freedom
>   for prisoners,
> to give sight to the blind,
> to free everyone
>   who suffers,
> ¹⁹ and to say, 'This is the year
>   the Lord has chosen.'"

²⁰ Jesus closed the book, then handed it back to the man in charge and sat down. Everyone in the meeting place looked straight at Jesus.

²¹ Then Jesus said to them, "What you have just heard me read has come true today."

²² All the people started talking about Jesus and were amazed at the wonderful things he said. They kept on asking, "Isn't he Joseph's son?"

²³ Jesus aswered:

"You will certainly want to tell me this saying, 'Doctor, first make yourself well.' You will tell me to do the same things here in my own hometown that you heard I did in Capernaum. ²⁴ But you can be sure that no prophets are liked by the people of their own hometown."

Luke 4.16-24

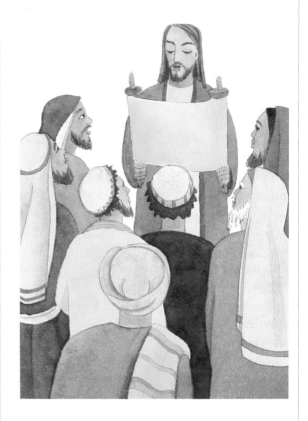

UNDERSTANDING THE TEXT

1. Look at the passage from Isaiah that Jesus read. List the people or groups he talks about. Write next to each person or group the condition that will change for them.

2. What does Jesus say that shows us that the text from Isaiah is not just a memory from the past?

3. Look up the following phrase in the glossary: *the year the Lord has chosen (YEAR OF FAVOR)*.

NAZARETH

For many years Jesus lived his daily life in peace according to the traditions of his village. Why then, did Jesus have to leave his peaceful life in Nazareth? What motivated him? Who did he think he was? Tongues were wagging and criticism abounded! It's always the same when, in our family or hometown, we shake up the traditional ways of thinking, acting and practicing religion. Often even those closest to us don't understand that we take this gospel seriously and that we really want to follow it. Sometimes people point their fingers and say, "Who does she think she is?" or "Is he trying to be better than everybody else?"

GOD'S PROJECT

It's official! It's public knowledge! It's true! Jesus has carried out God's mission. What Jesus said and did started to establish this happiness that comes from God. He was ready to give his life for this. What good news! Women and men, especially the poorest, have to wait no longer. God is interested in hearing their stories and their dreams. God is going to make it possible for them to taste the joy that has been denied them. This is God's promise!

BEING A CHRISTIAN

Being a Christian means believing, with Jesus Christ, that men and women are saved and freed from whatever was holding them captive. It means working so that God's happiness can be known by all who are trapped by suffering. It means doing, with Jesus Christ, actions that save, that free, and that give hope back to humanity; things that allow people to stand up straight, worthy and proud, as beloved daughters and sons of God. Being a Christian, believing in Christ, means being, like Jesus, someone who proclaims and lives the Good News.

AN ANNOUNCEMENT

*Words, Lord,
are so easy to say —
they don't cost anything.
They happen all by themselves.
We can say them
and then turn away without doing
anything for our brothers and sisters!*

*That's why, Lord, this time,
I won't speak! But I will console
the person who is trapped by pain.
I will stand up for the person
at whom others laugh.
I will open the door to joy
for the person who is walled in
by sadness.
I will welcome without judging
the person who is cast aside,
whom no one loves.
I will give what I have
to the person who is hungry
and who has nothing,
even if it is only my smile
and the comfort of my presence.*

*I won't talk, Lord,
but I will proclaim your love!
Lord Jesus Christ,
make me Good News for my sisters
and brothers of this world!*

JESUS IS CALLING

IN JESUS' DAY

Here we are, on the shores of the Sea of Galilee. In fact, it's not a sea, but a beautiful lake filled with clear water and fish. It is about 13 miles long and 6 miles wide. It is surrounded by green hills on one side, and the desert-like mountains of Syria on the other.

Jesus was preaching his message. But he didn't want to do it alone. To help him, he didn't choose famous and important people. He called ordinary folk — fishermen from the shores of the lake. Their names were Simon (who would be named Peter), Andrew, James, and John. They were the first apostles. They treasured in their hearts the words of Jesus, "I will teach you how to bring in people instead of fish."

WHEN THE GOSPELS WERE WRITTEN

They really did become "fishers of people." For many years in Jerusalem, Palestine, Syria and Rome, the apostles proclaimed the Good News. Many people followed them. Their call and the quick answer they gave to this call is often described. Christians can understand that Simon Peter, Andrew, James and John are true apostles — called and sent by Jesus.

When Mark wrote the following passage, James and perhaps Peter had already been killed for following Jesus — James in Palestine in the year 44 A.D. and Peter in Rome under Nero, between 64 and 67 A.D. Mark wasn't called directly by Jesus like the four fishermen. But he traveled with Peter for a long time and passed on his teaching to others.

THE GOSPEL

¹⁴ After John was arrested, Jesus went to Galilee and told the good news that comes from God. ¹⁵ He said, "The time has come! God's kingdom will soon be here. Turn back to God and believe the good news!"

¹⁶ As Jesus was walking along the shore of Lake Galilee, he saw Simon and his brother Andrew. They were fishermen and were casting their nets into the lake. ¹⁷ Jesus said to them, "Come with me! I will teach you how to bring in people instead of fish." ¹⁸ Right then the two brothers dropped their nets and went with him.

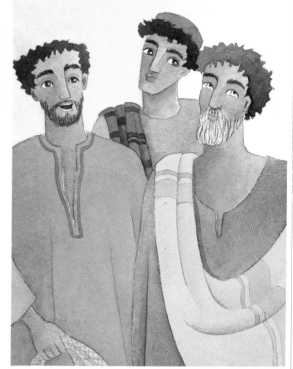

¹⁹ Jesus walked on and soon saw James and John, the sons of Zebedee. They were in a boat, mending their nets. ²⁰ At once Jesus asked them to come with him. They left their father in the boat with he hired workers and went with him.

Mark 1.14-20

UNDERSTANDING THE TEXT

1. What are the relationships of the first apostles to each other? Which ones have the same trade? Which ones are from the same family?

2. What and whom do they leave behind?

3. What do they find?

LIVING
TODAY

CHAPTER 7
JESUS
IS CALLING

To call

When we need someone for a difficult job or mission, we call her name as if to say, "Stop what you're doing. Come here!" We let him or her know. We think that this person has the necessary qualities to succeed at the job we want to give him or her. We say that this person is able to do it and will give everything to the mission. We trust this person totally. But will this person say yes?

To answer

The person who is called has some questions: "Am I good enough for this mission? Why was I called? Can I do it? Others are better suited than I am! What if I'm wrong?" But this person takes the chance, hopes to be worthy and answers with confidence, "You want me? Here I am. I'm coming!" Of course there will be difficulties. But the person who is called is not alone. Others have been called also. They can teach and encourage each other, and give one another support. Together they will give their life-energy, their love and their time because they know that it will bring joy to others.

We are all apostles

God calls each one of us. God doesn't call the holiest, the best, the smartest, the best dressed, or those who have sinned the least! In God's eyes we are all messengers, able to proclaim the Good News. Jesus' friends were all called, without exception, to be apostles — each one in his way, with the specific gifts of body or mind; each one with his job and life! Students, mothers, professors, fathers, forest rangers, children, workers, technicians, employees or farmers — we are all chosen by God to make God's love visible to all living creatures.

Each one of us, by what we do, is called to proclaim the Good News of Jesus, who came to free humanity from its captivity.

5
4

HERE WE ARE

*How can the world
hear the Good News
of God's tenderness
if there is no one to open arms
to those who are hurt
and exhausted by life's misery?*

*How can the world
look at God in wonder
if there is no one
to accomplish marvelous acts
of love, peace and sharing
in God's name?*

*How can the world
hear the Good News
of God's forgiveness,
if there is no one
to forget hate
and extend hands
beyond bitterness?*

*Here we are, God,
ready to proclaim your Good News.
Here we are;
make us your disciples!*

CHAPTER 8
THE PARALYZED MAN FROM CAPERNAUM

IN JESUS' DAY

Jesus was starting to be known. Crowds followed him through Galilee. They talked of what he did. Jesus arrived in Capernaum, which was Peter and Andrew's hometown. They had a house there. People crowded around the house that Jesus had entered. There was no room to move.

At one point four men arrived at the house carrying a paralyzed man on a stretcher. They tried to get close to Jesus. When they couldn't get through the crowds, they took the outside staircase up to the rooftop. Then they made a hole in the roof (that was made of wood and packed mud), and lowered the paralyzed man down to Jesus. Jesus forgave the man's sins and healed him. Remember that sickness and sin were tied together in the minds of the people of Jesus' day.

WHEN THE GOSPELS WERE WRITTEN

The memory of the healings that Jesus performed remained alive for a long time in the villages where they took place. Storytellers reminded everyone of them during evening get-togethers. It was probably Mark who gathered these stories of Jesus' healings and placed them in his gospel.

Mark emphasizes the condemnation that some religious leaders had in their hearts: "Jesus is blasphemous because only God can forgive sins." And Mark points out the criticisms expressed to the first Christians: "You consider Jesus to be God."

It is especially important for Mark to show that Jesus gave us a new way of seeing God — a God who is close to human beings, who heals their bodies and hearts. The healing of the paralyzed man is much more than the simple gesture of a healer of that time. It shows that Jesus, "the Son of Man," forgives and heals with God's power.

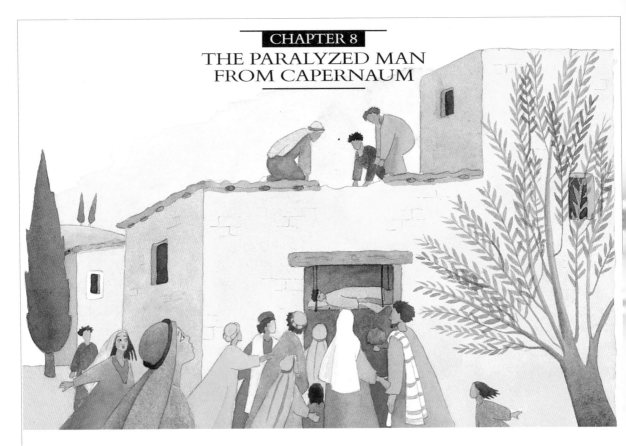

CHAPTER 8
THE PARALYZED MAN FROM CAPERNAUM

THE GOSPEL

[1] Jesus went back to Capernaum, and a few days later people heard that he was at home. [2] Then so many of them came to the house that there wasn't even standing room left in front of the door.

Jesus was still teaching [3] when four people came up, carrying a crippled man on a mat. [4] But because of the crowd, they could not get him to Jesus. So they made a hole in the roof above him and let the man down in front of everyone.

[5] When Jesus saw how much faith they had, he said to the crippled man, "My friend, your sins are forgiven."

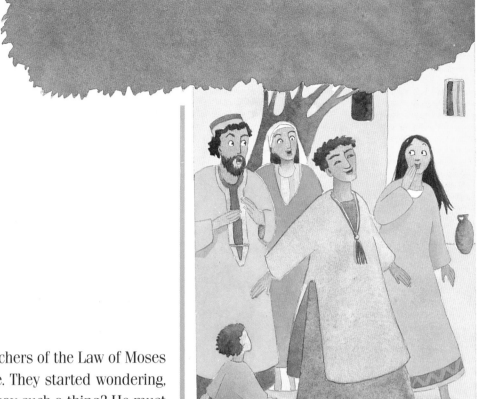

⁶ Some of the teachers of the Law of Moses were sitting there. They started wondering, ⁷ "Why would he say such a thing? He must think he is God! Only God can forgive sins."

⁸ Right away, Jesus knew what they were thinking, and he said, "Why are you thinking such things? ⁹ Is it easier for me to tell this crippled man that his sins are forgiven or to tell him to get up and pick up his mat and go on home? ¹⁰ I will show you that the Son of Man has the right to forgive sins here on earth." So Jesus said to the man, ¹¹ "Get up! Pick up your mat and go on home."

¹² The man got right up. He picked up his mat and went out while everyone watched in amazement. They praised God and said, "We have never seen anything like this!"

Mark 2.1-12

UNDERSTANDING THE TEXT

1. Look for Capernaum on the map.

2. Read the ancient story of this miracle as a storyteller might tell it (verses 1 to 5 and 11 to 12).

3. Then read all of what Mark writes. What do verses 6 to 10 add to the story?

4. What is the new "title" that Jesus gives to himself in this story? Look up its meaning in the glossary.

THE PARALYZED MAN
FROM CAPERNAUM

Paralyzed

Some peoples' bodies are paralyzed by sickness. To move around they have to ask for help. But, even though they depend on others to move, they are still independent people — able to love, to create and to make decisions. There are other ways a person can be paralyzed — when a person is wrongly labeled and given a bad reputation; when someone can't live without others pointing their fingers and laughing.

We are also paralyzed by evil — when we allow our desires to control us; when we don't try to get out of the state of sin in which we are rooted; when we don't make any efforts to bring happiness; when we turn away from God. Jesus calls us to "move" and to stand up against everything that paralyzes.

Forgiving

When we are forgiven, God doesn't just say, "I cast away your sin. I continue to love you!" When we are forgiven, God lifts up the person who is hardened by sin, attached to evil. God helps that person emerge from the shadows in which he or she has hidden, far from God and others. God sets the sinners "on their feet" and encourages them to walk toward the light where joy and love are given as Jesus gave them. God always answers the person who asks for help to break free from the sin that paralyzes!

Opening the Roof

God loves people! God wants us to be happy and free. This Good News comes to every house, to every place where people live. It even breaks down walls! Nothing can resist this Good News, not even those who would like to hold it back and keep it from reaching people's hearts. If someone tries to block the way, the Good News that heals, reveals, and frees will find another road!

LIFT US UP

*Lord, lift us up
from sadness
that makes us focus
only on ourselves,
from laziness
that surrounds us
with its lukewarm approach,
from cowardice
that turns our eyes
away from someone
at whom others laugh,
from sin
that wants to bind us
by leading us
down easy roads,
from nasty looks
or mean words
that someone showed us
or said to us out of cruelty,
from selfishness
that makes us forget
our sisters and brothers
who don't have bread or hope,
from such overwhelming sadness
that it takes away our strength.
Lift us up, Lord!
We will go forward
in life with you by our side.*

CHAPTER 9

JESUS AND LEVI

IN JESUS' DAY

Tax collectors were not well liked in Israel. They were called "publicans." People accused them of getting rich unfairly — of collecting more taxes than the government required and of keeping the difference for themselves. Pharisees accused them of being unclean (sinful) because they were often around pagan foreigners. They were seen as sinners.

But Jesus did something astonishing. He called a tax collector (a publican) named Levi, son of Alphaeus, to follow him. Levi organized a dinner at his house with some of his friends who were also tax collectors. Jesus and his disciples were invited. The scribes who sided with the Pharisees found this to be scandalous, "We won't eat with such people!" Jesus explained, "I didn't come to invite good people to be my followers. I came to invite sinners."

This Levi, who followed Jesus, is none other than Matthew who wrote the gospel that bears his name.

WHEN THE GOSPEL WAS WRITTEN

After Jesus' death and resurrection, Christians often got together to eat, pray and remember Jesus. Soon, however, problems arose. During these gatherings, often the rich people had good seats, and the poor were put at the end of the table. Also, certain Christians of Jewish origin refused to share the meal with Christians of non-Jewish origin.

Jesus' example of eating with tax collectors and sinners — told in the gospels — helped the first Christians to understand that they were all called to eat together around the same table.

Before God, there is no discrimination between Jews and non-Jews, slave and free persons, men and women.

THE GOSPEL

¹³ Once again, Jesus went to the shore of Lake Galilee. A large crowd gathered around him, and he taught them. ¹⁴ As he walked along, he saw Levi, the son of Alphaeus. Levi was sitting at the place for paying taxes, and Jesus said to him, "Come with me!" So he got up and went with Jesus.

¹⁵ Later, Jesus and his disciples were having dinner at Levi's house. Many tax collectors and other sinners had become followers of Jesus, and they were also guests at the dinner.

¹⁶ Some of the teachers of the Law of Moses were Pharisees, and they saw that Jesus was eating with sinners and tax collectors. So they asked his disciples, "Why does he eat with tax collectors and sinners?"

¹⁷ Jesus heard them and answered, "Healthy people don't need a doctor, but sick people do. I didn't come to invite good people to be my followers. I came to invite sinners."

Mark 2.13-17

UNDERSTANDING THE TEXT

1. Write the names of the following people or groups of people in two columns:
- those who are for Jesus
- those who are against him.

2. Do you know of other people who were called by Jesus? What were their occupations?

3. In this passage the evangelist quotes a proverb. Try to find it.

4. Look up the meaning of the following words in the glossary: *good people (righteous)* and *sinner*.

LIVING TODAY

THE GOOD PEOPLE

No one is entirely righteous. Only one person has ever been entirely righteous: Jesus Christ. Only Jesus, throughout his whole life, loved God and others with all his strength, body and mind. We'd say for everyone else, "They try to be good!" They try to live their lives respecting others and being faithful to God's call. Being good — being righteous — doesn't mean receiving a medal or being handed a plaque to hang on the wall! When God declares that we are good, it is because he transforms us and give us the strength to live according to the Gospel.

SINNERS

Everyone is a sinner. We all let sin get the best of us at times. We let sin lead us on ways that have nothing to do with love for God and others. To be a sinner is to lead a life that is far from the Gospel. In God's eyes no human being is a prisoner of sin forever. Jesus came to help us fight against the forces of evil so that we might be freed from their chains.

THE "GOOD" AND THE "BAD"

We like to categorize others, to classify them, to give them labels. "She's a saint! He's a sinner!" In this way we can judge and reject people without compassion. "I can hang around him. But she's no good; we'd better avoid her." We have a hard time admitting that others can change! There are whole groups of people who are labeled "good" or "bad," once and for all. Do we who judge forget that we too are both saints and sinners?

NO ONE IS LEFT OUT

In Jesus' eyes no one is excluded and no one should be condemned. For him, people are to be loved. Jesus calls each of us to stand up and experience God's love. Jesus helps us understand that God invites everyone into the Kingdom and he never refuses his tenderness to those who turn to him and respond to Jesus' call.

THE SAINTS AND THE SINNERS

Who can trust us, Lord?

Sometimes we snap,
ready to bite;
sometimes we smile,
ready to caress;
sometimes we deceive with lies,
sometimes we speak the truth
without fear of being
judged unfairly.

Sometimes we sing your praises
as if there were only you;
sometimes we set you aside
as if you didn't count.

Sometimes we cry out
to change the world;
sometimes we stay in our corner
without lifting a finger;
sometimes we keep everything
just for ourselves,
sometimes we run with open arms
to give everything away!

This is how we are, Lord —
saints and sinners!
But you trust us!
You call us!
You offer us the possibility
of letting our hidden light shine!

CHAPTER 10

PICKING GRAINS OF WHEAT

IN JESUS' DAY

Traditionally, in Israel, the Sabbath was a day of rest (like our Sunday). In Jesus' day this had already been a law for over a thousand years, going back to Moses. The law existed to help men and women, slaves and masters, to live more happily and freely. It was time to rest, relax, reflect and pray after six days of work.

But in Jesus' day things changed. The Pharisees had a lot of influence. What mattered was the Law. The Pharisees wrote lists of everything that could not be done on the Sabbath — planting, harvesting, reaping, milling grain, writing two letters of the alphabet, sewing two stitches, lighting or putting out a lamp. People were becoming slaves to the Sabbath law.

Pharisees were always asking themselves, "Does the Law allow this?" Jesus, on the other hand, asked, "What do the people need? Are they sick? Cold?

Hungry?" Jesus often disagreed with the Pharisees. They accused him of not respecting the Law.

WHEN THE GOSPELS WERE WRITTEN

The early Christians remembered how free Jesus was about the Law. They themselves observed the ritual Jewish law less and less. They understood much better that Jesus, the Son of Man, was Lord and Master of the Law. They had confrontations with the Pharisees and were often persecuted by them.

Mark's story of "picking grains of wheat" shows how much the first Christians remembered Jesus defending his starving disciples against the Pharisees and the Law.

THE GOSPEL

^{23} One Sabbath Jesus and his disciples were walking through some wheat fields. His disciples were picking grains of wheat as they went along. ^{24} Some Pharisees asked Jesus, "Why are your disciples picking grain on the Sabbath? They are not supposed to do that!"

^{25} Jesus answered, "Haven't you read what David did when he and his followers were hungry and in need? ^{26} It was during the time of Abiathar the high priest. David went into the house of God and ate the sacred loaves of bread that only priests are allowed to eat. He also gave some to his followers."

^{27} Jesus finished by saying, "People were not made for the good of the Sabbath. The Sabbath was made for the good of people. ^{28} So the Son of Man is Lord over the Sabbath."

Mark 2.23–28

UNDERSTANDING THE TEXT

1. Look for all the words that talk about food and all the words that talk about the Law.

2. What written document is Jesus talking about when he says, "Haven't you read what...?"

3. How does Jesus express his thoughts in verse 27? How would the Pharisees phrase this?

LIVING TODAY

LAWS

We can't get along without laws. They are necessary because they help ensure that peoples' rights are respected. They allow us to live together. Laws exist to help us live more freely by keeping in mind the freedom and rights of others. These laws are designed to serve people. There are also "laws" that are designed to help us love God and respond to God's love. Everyone must decide either to live by these "laws" or not. God doesn't force anyone. These laws, which give us some guidelines, help people find their way to God more easily and live in God's love. "Human laws" and "God's laws" are intended for everyone's well being.

HUNGER

All around the world, men, women and children are hungry. Many die because they don't have enough food to survive. So what choice do we have? Shouldn't we do everything possible so people don't starve to death anymore? Can we live with much more than we need while others die because they have nothing? Sharing becomes a duty, a law for everyone!

Can we be complacent singing and praying to God while other children of God live in misery? Can we love God without also loving our neighbor who is starving? Sharing with the hungry and helping them live with human dignity is a law for all those who claim to love God!

We have been freed in Jesus! We live our lives rooted in the love of God and not in fear of being punished by God. In Jesus we learn to make choices based on love, not obligation. With Jesus we understand that our neighbor's life is more important in God's eyes than all the laws in the world. For Jesus there is only one law that summarizes all the others, "Love God and love your neighbor."

FREE TO LOVE

I am not praying, Lord,
because I have to.
I pray because I love you
and I don't want to live my life
without talking to you
and listening to you.
You are my sunshine!

I don't worship you in Church
because I have to.
I go because you love us
and because in Church
you nourish us and surround us
with your presence.
Lord, how could I live
without receiving signs
of the great tenderness
you have for all people?

I don't give to others
because it is a commandment.
I give because my brothers
and sisters are living in misery
and because they need my help
in order to live with dignity.

Lord, when we love
we don't measure things
out anymore. We are free!
Teach us, Lord,
to do everything with love.

JESUS AND THE TWELVE

IN JESUS' DAY

Jesus didn't work alone. He called together a team to work with him. Jesus' team was made up of twelve people (the number twelve being a reminder of the twelve tribes of Israel, or all of Israel). Twelve meant totality. The Twelve were called to travel with Jesus and then to be sent to far off places. Peter was the leader of the group. Judas was in charge of the money. The Twelve stayed with Jesus until his arrest. Then they scattered for a while.

The Twelve were not alone. With them there was a bigger group of seventy-two disciples who are often forgotten. At the risk of shocking the people of his day, Jesus was also followed by a group of women — Mary Magdalene; Joanna, wife of Chuza; Susanna; and others (Luke 8.2, 3). Unlike the Twelve, the women followed Jesus all the way to the cross!

WHEN THE GOSPELS WERE WRITTEN

After Jesus' death and resurrection, the Twelve (except Judas, the traitor) regained some courage. Now that Jesus was gone, they understood in a new way what it meant "to be with him" and "to be sent by him." Everything depended on them. They were to carry the Good News to the far reaches of the world.

They were helped by others, especially for material needs. A group of seven deacons formed. New disciples, such as Paul, challenged them to be more daring. Women played a very important role in welcoming Christian groups into their homes.

In the early communities, when the text was read that told of how the Twelve were called, Christians understood that their leaders were sent by Jesus. When they heard that Jesus "instituted the Twelve," they understood better that they, too, were part of this new creation.

THE GOSPEL

¹³ Jesus decided to ask some of his disciples to go up on a mountain with him, and they went. ¹⁴ Then he chose twelve of them to be his apostles, so that they could be with him. He also wanted to send them out to preach ¹⁵ and to force out demons. ¹⁶ Simon was one of the twelve, and Jesus named him Peter. ¹⁷ There were also James and John, the two sons of Zebedee. Jesus called them Boanerges, which means "Thunderbolts."

¹⁸ Andrew,
Philip,
Bartholomew,
Matthew,
Thomas,
James son of Alphaeus,
and Thaddaeus were also apostles.
The others were Simon,
known as the Eager One,
¹⁹ and Judas Iscariot, who later betrayed Jesus.

Mark 3.13-19

UNDERSTANDING THE TEXT

1. What was Jesus' goal when he formed the group called "the Twelve"?

2. In the list of the Twelve,
some of the names are already familiar to you.
What do you know about
Peter, John, James, Andrew and Matthew?

3. Why do you think that Jesus didn't want to act alone?

4. What is an "Eager One" (Zealot)?
Look up the word in the glossary.

A TEAM

Someone who wants to carry out a big project surrounds himself or herself with a carefully chosen team. The "team members" gather around the one who thought of the project — they listen to this person and watch him or her outline the plans. They find the project so fascinating that nothing seems more important than seeing it through to the end. So they set everything else aside to give themselves entirely to the project.

A DIVERSE TEAM

What good are intelligent people if there is no one to coordinate their knowledge or skills? In the team, all the members use their individual talents for the good of the project. If the team includes many different people, ideas and methods of acting, then it is better able to fulfill its mission by constantly adjusting to find the best way to carry out the project. The one who gathered the team together calls on the individual talents of each member.

A PLACE FOR EVERYONE

Women, men and children — Jesus called them all to take their place on his team, "Come, follow me!" Each place is unique and important. To be part of his team, Jesus asks us to listen to his Word, live by his gospel and join with the others who are sent.

A GOOD NEWS TEAM

Christians are the Good News team — called and sent by Jesus. Their task is to carry out his wonderful project: to proclaim through words and actions that God loves the entire world. God trusts men and women with the Good News.

WORK

You are looking for workers, Lord?

Workers to send out
to pray even for our enemies,
to forgive those who sin,
to use the power of gentleness,
to love our neighbor
as much as we love ourselves?

Workers to create justice,
to give joy and happiness freely,
to share our daily bread,
to stay with those
who have been abandoned?

Workers to support
people going through hard times,
to open doors
to people who are left outside
in misery and poverty,
to clothe people
who have nothing to wear,
to visit the sick,
to tell everyone the Good News
that God loves us?

You are looking for workers?
This is a job for us, Lord.
We are coming!

CHAPTER 12

THE BEATITUDES

IN JESUS' DAY

Jesus decided to talk to ordinary people. He met a lot of poor people — peasants who were burdened by taxes, sick people who were abandoned by society, people who were mourning the loss of a dear friend or relative, beggars, slaves and widows without any income. These people hardly dared to hope for a change in their situation. They were not happy. Jesus told them, "It will change! You will be, and you are already, blessed!"

Jesus also met people who were very generous, who shared and who believed in justice. Some were even in prison because their words and actions displeased the leaders. Jesus also told them the same thing, "You are happy, you will be happy! Are you not, like me, carrying out what the prophets had done?"

WHEN THE GOSPELS WERE WRITTEN

Jesus' teachings, probably given on several occasions, were gathered together and updated by Matthew at a later date. They are found in the passage called "the Beatitudes," which means "blessed with happiness." Luke wrote another shorter version, which is a little harsher. He added unhappy predictions for those who stray from the gospel (Luke 6.20-26).

Toward the end of the first century, poverty hadn't disappeared. Quite the opposite! After four years of war between the Jews and the Romans (from 66 to 70 A.D.), thousands were dead or in prison. Cities and the countryside lay in ruins. More than ever before it was important to share, make peace and work for justice.

Also at this time, Christians were being persecuted. They were hunted, dragged before the courts, tortured and executed because they believed in justice and in Jesus' message.

It is important to think of these poor and persecuted people when we read Matthew's Beatitudes, which were written for them. But not only for them.

THE GOSPEL

¹ When Jesus saw the crowds, he went up on the side of a mountain and sat down.

Jesus' disciples gathered around him, ² and he taught them:

³ God blesses those people
who depend only on him.
They belong to the kingdom
of heaven!

⁴ God blesses those people
who grieve.
They will find comfort!

⁵ God blesses those people
who are humble.
The earth will belong
to them!

⁶ God blesses those people
who want to obey him
more than to eat or drink.
They will be given
what they want!

⁷ God blesses those people
who are merciful.
They will be treated
with mercy!

⁸ God blesses those people
whose hearts are pure.
They will see him!

⁹ God blesses those people
who make peace.
They will be called
his children!

¹⁰ God blesses those people
who are treated badly
for doing right.
They belong to the kingdom
of heaven.

¹¹ God will bless you when people insult you, mistreat you, and tell all kinds of evil lies about you because of me. ¹² Be happy and excited! You will have a great reward in heaven. People did these same things to the prophets who lived long ago.

Matthew 5.1-12

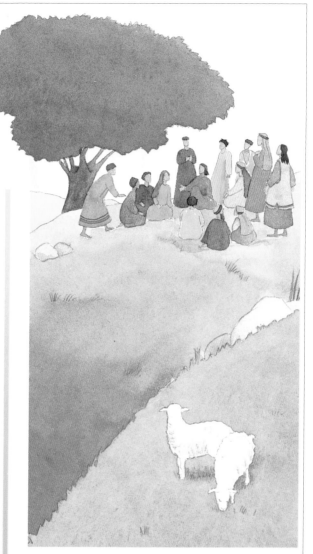

UNDERSTANDING THE TEXT

1. There are three parts in each Beatitude: the expression "God blesses"; the people who are said to be blessed; and the reason why these people are or will be blessed. Try to find these three parts.

2. Look at the Beatitudes that are in the present tense and those that are in the future tense. Where are those that are in the present tense (at the beginning, end or in the middle?) Why are they placed there?

3. What are the two reasons that Matthew gives for being insulted and mistreated?

Happiness

All women and men everywhere are searching for happiness. Happiness is food on the table each day. Happiness is a house in which to live. It's money to spend. It's a world with room for everybody. Happiness is being consoled when life is too hard. It's laughter and not just sadness. It's having justice on your side. It's loving and being loved. Happiness is having generous people around you. It's trust, freely given without fear of betrayal. It's peace to build, have children and work without fear of bombs and guns. Happiness is the right to think, act and speak freely. It's the right to believe in God without being chased or ridiculed. It's the joy of knowing God. And it's more. God wants happiness for all people!

Broken happiness

There are many poor people in our world. Entire countries! They don't have food to eat, land to farm, jobs or money. Often we don't help these people find ways out of this poverty. Sometimes, when we have a lot, we prefer to enjoy our own riches and even increase them, even if it means neglecting or taking advantage of those who have nothing. How many tears and how much unhappiness are caused by poverty? Many people are persecuted — because of their faith, ideas or religion, or because they upset the leaders of their country. There are many victims of violence — wars, exile, uprisings, shootings, domestic violence. Many people have their happiness ruined by other people. It seems as if some people want to prevent others from being happy, or that they want to keep everything for themselves and not leave anything for others!

Living the beatitudes

Around the world generous men and women don't just stand watching this happen. They work to bring about the happiness that God wants for all of God's children. They make peace, live with justice, defend human dignity, give freely, act in truth, work to eliminate hunger, and fight for human rights. They don't look for happiness in money. Instead they try to build a friendly earth; they live the Beatitudes. This is how Christians must put into practice their love of God and their faith in Jesus Christ — by living the Beatitudes.

THE EARTH

Be happy, my friends.
God joins us
in our fight against misery
and helps us distribute the food
that we have harvested
throughout the earth!

Be happy, my friends.
God comes with us
to fight against violence
with power and gentleness,
and to bring laughter
to all those who cry
in fear and abandonment!

Be happy, my friends.
God comes with us
to bring justice
to those who have no voice,
and to fill those who have nothing
more to hope for with tenderness!

Be happy, my friends.
God comes with us
to end war and bring our hands
together in a great circle of peace!

Be happy, my friends.
God comes with us
to create a world filled
with joy!

CHAPTER 13

LIGHT AND SALT

IN JESUS' DAY

When Jesus spoke he didn't use words that were hard to understand. He used words that were clear to everyone. He used examples from everyday life: salt and light. Salt gives taste to food. One candle, placed on a stand, will light up a whole room. But hidden under a basket it will go out and is of no use. Jesus' disciples understood what he meant when he told them, "You are like salt for everyone on earth... You are like light for the whole world!"

What Jesus said wasn't like what the religious leaders said. He didn't repeat clichés. Instead, he knew what he was saying and was speaking with authority. He said new things. For example, "You were told: 'You shall not kill.' But I, Jesus, say to you, 'Make peace with your enemies!'"

WHEN THE GOSPELS WERE WRITTEN

Matthew's gospel was written a few decades after Jesus was crucified. It was written for the Christians of Palestine and Syria. Many of them had converted from Judaism. Most of them had not met Jesus.

In these communities the excitement of the early years had subsided. Their faith was less vibrant. Some thought that, to be a Christian, it was enough just to pray. Some had already been persecuted. Others were afraid. The opponents continued to teach. Christian communities risked becoming complacent and self-serving.

Matthew's gospel tries to wake them up, "By your actions, you must be like the salt of the earth and the light of the world! You are not here for yourselves, but for others! Jesus calls you to be different from others through the love that you show for everyone, even your enemies!"

THE GOSPEL

¹³ You are like salt for everyone on earth. But if salt no longer tastes like salt, how can it make food salty? All it is good for is to be thrown out and walked on.

¹⁴ You are like light for the whole world. A city built on top of a hill cannot be hidden, ¹⁵ and no one would light a lamp and put it under a clay pot. A lamp is placed on a lamp-stand, where it can give light to everyone in the house. ¹⁶ Make your light shine, so that others will see the good that you do and will praise your Father in heaven...

⁴³ You have heard people say, "Love your neighbors and hate your enemies." ⁴⁴ But I tell you to love your enemies and pray for anyone who mistreats you. ⁴⁵ Then you will be acting like your Father in heaven. He makes the sun rise on both good and bad people. And he sends rain for the ones who do right and for the ones who do wrong. ⁴⁶ If you love only those people who love you, will God reward you for that? Even tax collectors love their friends. ⁴⁷ If you greet only your friends, what's so great about that? Don't even unbelievers do that? ⁴⁸ But you must always act like your Father in heaven.

Matthew 5.13-16; 43-48

UNDERSTANDING THE TEXT

1. Look for the word "everyone" and "others" in verses 13 to 16.
What are the two actions that are mentioned?
Why are the two attitudes so different?

2. What reason do Jesus' disciples have for being salt and light?

3. How must Christians be different from non-believers?

LIVING TODAY

THEY ARE LIGHT

People notice Christians! Not because they are smarter than other people, or because they act smarter, and not because they say proudly, "We know everything! We know how to live like people of God! We are the best! We know God! We know how to talk to God!" Where Christians are present, darkness should vanish — lies and hypocrisy, greed, domination, overwhelming envy and a lack of compassion. Where Christians are present, there should be more light, as if the light grows with each act of sharing, each word of forgiveness, each time peace is sought after and each time a poor person is cared for. Then people would say, "Look! There is light here! Maybe Christ's friends are here?"

THEY ADD FLAVOR

At times people lose their desire to live; they have nothing left to look forward to. "What good is living," they say, "if things will never change? If the strong keep dominating the weak? If the world turns its back on people in need? If death has the final word?" At times people live like machines, working to get as much money as possible and forgetting other people. Like robots that have no feeling. Where Christians are present, life should taste better! The joy of living should be sweet like a meadow in summer! Hope should rise like the morning sun and sing that evil is conquered and that death has lost! Surprise should be seen on people's faces because of the joy of being and working together to bring about such wonderful things! Then people would say, "Look! Life has a lot of flavor, like when we salt our food! Maybe Christ's friends are here?"

A DISTINCT SIGN

How can we recognize Christians? Because they wear a cross? Because they pray? Because they go to church? Where Christians are present, there should be no more distinction between people we love and people we hate, people we welcome and people we ignore, people we hang around and people we avoid! There should be understanding even if we don't agree, mutual respect despite our different nationalities. A welcome for everyone and a desire to build a world together. Then people would say, "Look! There is love here, and people are even talking to their enemies! Christ's friends certainly are here!"

PERFECT

*Isn't it enough, God, to kneel
before you, to sing praises
to your name and to pray
with all our hearts, if we want
to be your "perfect" children?*

*Lord, you ask us
to love those
we don't want to love,
to hold out our hands
to those who have drawn away,
to get close to those
who hurt us by their words
or actions, to reach out to those
who reject us,
and to lay the first stone
in the bridge of forgiveness!*

*It is harder to be your child
than it is to bow down
before you and worship you
with all our hearts!*

*This is why we are asking you,
our heavenly God,
to teach us how to love your way,
so we can become your children
in this world!*

CHAPTER 14

JESUS' PRAYER

IN JESUS' DAY

Praying was part of everyday life. Every devout Jew prayed twice a day, when the offering was made at the Temple: at 9 a.m. and 3 p.m. Jews knew many prayers. One of them contained 18 petitions. The Jews prayed to "Our Father in heaven." They asked for "enough food." They prayed for "the reign of God to come." It was often thought that the coming of this reign would end the Roman occupation.

Some, especially the Pharisees, liked to pray in public so that other people would think better of them. They were admired as they stood in public squares or in the synagogues. This made them happy.

Jesus learned to pray as a young child, at home and in the synagogue. He knew the Jewish prayers. He read the Psalms. As an adult, when Jesus was traveling through Palestine, he would pause sometimes to be alone to talk privately to God on a mountain or in the desert.

Jesus' disciples saw him pray. Jesus taught them how to talk to God. It wasn't important to repeat lots of noisy formulas so that God would do as they wanted. Instead, it was important to find out what God wanted *them* to do! This is how Jesus acted throughout his whole life.

He also taught his disciples some prayers to memorize. He chose these from among many Jewish prayers, and he simplified them. He also gave the prayers a deeper meaning.

WHEN THE GOSPELS WERE WRITTEN

The early Christians got together often to pray. They invented new prayers to Jesus, the Lord. But they also continued to use the traditional Jewish "formulas" to talk with God.

They didn't go to the synagogues any more. In 70 A.D. the Temple was destroyed by the Romans. The early Christians were in danger if they gathered in public, so they often met in someone's house to pray.

They remembered Jesus' life and understood that he lived in complete acceptance of God's will. Before his death Jesus had prayed, "Father, you can do anything. Don't make me suffer by having me drink from this cup. But do what you want, and not what I want" (Mark 14.36).

Sometimes they wondered, "How should we pray? What words should we use to talk to God?" Matthew and Luke taught them the Lord's prayer, beginning "Our Father." (Luke's version is a little bit shorter: Luke 11.2-4.) This prayer has become a prayer for all Christians. Over time the translation changed a little bit but the heart of the prayer is still there. Very early on Christians added an ending to the prayer: "The kingdom, the power, and the glory are yours forever. Amen."

CHAPTER 14
JESUS' PRAYER

THE GOSPEL

⁵ When you pray, don't be like those show-offs who love to stand up and pray in the meeting places and on the street corners. They do this just to look good. I can assure you that they already have their reward.

⁶ When you pray, go into a room alone and close the door. Pray to your Father in private. He knows what is done in private, and he will reward you.

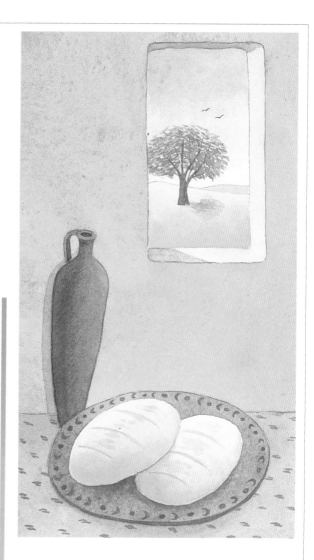

⁷ When you pray, don't talk on and on as people do who don't know God. They think God likes to hear long prayers. ⁸ Don't be like them. Your Father knows what you need before you ask.

⁹ You should pray like this:

Our Father in heaven,
help us to honor
    your name.
¹⁰ Come and set up
    your kingdom,
so that everyone on earth
    will obey you,
as you are obeyed
    in heaven.
¹¹ Give us our food for today.
¹² Forgive us for doing wrong,
    as we forgive others.
¹³ Keep us from being tempted
    and protect us from evil.

Matthew 6.5–13

UNDERSTANDING THE TEXT

1. In the prayer Jesus taught, there are petitions for God and petitions for ourselves.
Try to find them.

2. Compare the translation of the "Lord's prayer" on this page with the prayer we use today. Are there important differences?

3. Look for the prayer that Jesus said before his arrest (page 180) and on the cross (page 198).
Could you use these prayers in your life?

LIVING TODAY

GOD THE FATHER

Some people say that God is far away, or that we should be afraid of God like a powerful master who has no mercy on his servants, who punishes them severely, who looks only at what they do wrong, and who demands that they bow down in front of him. Some people also say that prayer is only good for avoiding God's anger. What a terrible mistake!

Thanks to Jesus the Son we truly see "who" God is — God is close to us as parents are close to their children; everything good parents do is designed only to help their children live in joy. Being a good parent means being interested in nothing more than the happiness of one's children; it also means being prepared for anything in order to do this! With God there is nothing to be afraid of; there is only love, to be given and received!

PRAYING TO GOD

When we pray we spend time with God. When we really love we want only one thing — to be with those we love, simply to feel the joy of being with them and to know that they always love. Praying is letting words flow from our hearts! Words that express our joy and sadness. Words that express cries of rebellion and calls for help when we don't understand life anymore and when we can't take it any longer. Words that express our fear before death and suffering. Words shared with God are like a conversation with a good friend, who knows us and always comes to our rescue.

Our whole life is carried in prayer. And God always listens!

PRAYING AND CHANGING

Praying isn't like a vending machine where we only have to put in a few coins to get what we want. We don't pray in order to get something in return! Or if we do, we only see God as a sort of giant bank or shopping mall!

Praying is turning to God as we turn toward the sun. Can we live without sunlight? When we pray we place ourselves in the light of God's love. We become more and more aware of God's great tenderness and we begin to change inside. We stop asking to pass our tests, to have good health or to be protected from accidents. We start, above all, to want to do God's will. God's will for us is to live as God's children, in Jesus' image, full of hospitality and forgiveness, full of love for God and for our brothers and sisters on earth. Prayer changes us. It makes us look at life, our world and other people with God's eyes. It opens us to God's Spirit and helps us act according to Jesus' gospel.

WORDS TO PRAY WITH

*There are words that everyone
knows and uses every day,
words that express our love,
"God our Father who is in heaven."
You are life;
you are tenderness!*

*They are words
that we have learned,
that are on our lips
and that sing in our hearts;
"Jesus, the Christ, Son of God!"
You are our brother;
you are the gospel!*

*They are words that are as light
as a breeze,
or that burn like a fire;
words that express our courage,
"Holy Spirit, breath of God!"
You are light;
you are freedom!*

*They are words
that wake us up,
that transform us
and that bring us to life;
they are words to pray with!
Oh, our Lord and God,
teach us to pray!*

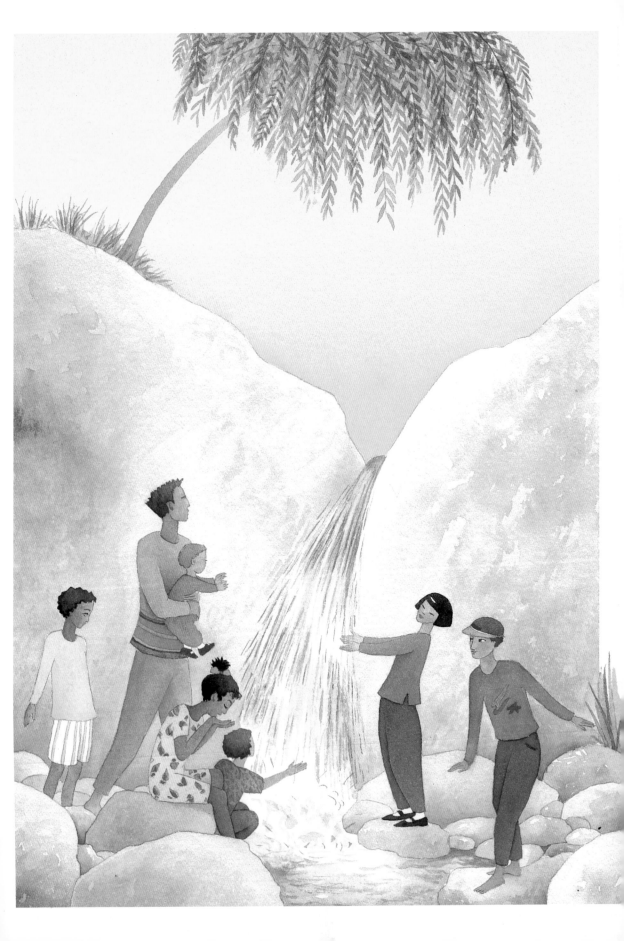

CHAPTER 15

THE SAMARITAN WOMAN

IN JESUS' DAY

To travel from Galilee to Jerusalem, Jesus and his followers had to travel through Samaria. It was the shortest route; it took only three days by foot to get there. But it wasn't the safest route because it meant going through an unfriendly country. Jews and Samaritans didn't talk to each other. They hated each other. Sometimes they even fought. But why?

It's an old story. Samaritans were a people of mixed ancestry: Jews and foreigners. For nine centuries Samaritans hadn't gone to the Temple in Jerusalem to pray. They worshiped God on a mountain called Mount Gerizim. They had their own priests, their own law and their own places of worship.

As they were crossing Samaria Jesus did something that everyone would remember. He spoke to one of the inhabitants of the country. That just wasn't done. Jesus spoke to a woman. That was done even less. He asked the woman for a favor. The disciples were shocked, but the Samaritans welcomed his Word.

All of this happened near a well that, at the time, was 18 centuries old. The same well exists today. It is 35 feet deep. The water isn't stagnant like the water found in ponds or cisterns. It runs cool and clear and comes from a source at the very bottom of the well.

WHEN THE GOSPELS WERE WRITTEN

John wrote his gospel probably in the 90's A.D. At that time, the Temple in Jerusalem no longer existed. The Good News had been proclaimed with much success by Philip, a deacon, in Samaria. It had reached the ends of the known world. It was like "living water" that flowed without ceasing.

John wrote his story from his memories of Jesus' meeting with the Samaritan woman. He wanted to illustrate three things:

- that Jesus, through his example, broke down barriers between Jews and Samaritans;

- that Samaritans discovered who Jesus was little by little: a person who was thirsty, a prophet, the Messiah, or Christ, and even the Savior of the world;

- that Christians who heard this story could learn to see Jesus as the Samaritan woman did and therefore discover this Jesus who offers living water.

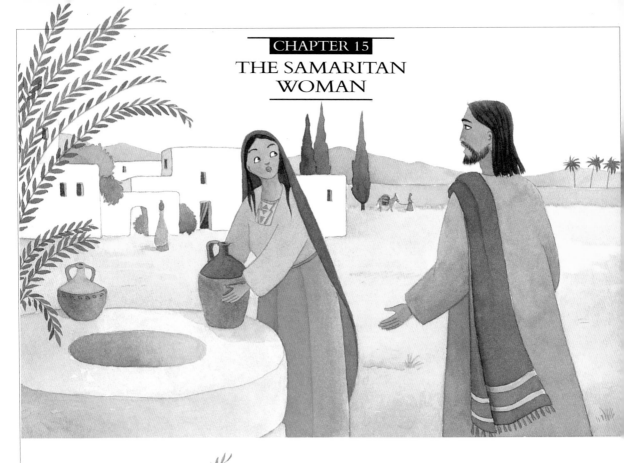

THE GOSPEL

[3] Jesus left Judea and started for Galilee again. [4] This time he had to go through Samaria, [5] and on his way he came to the town of Sychar. It was near the field that Jacob had long ago given to his son Joseph. [6-8] The well that Jacob had dug was still there, and Jesus sat down beside it because he was tired from traveling. It was noon, and after Jesus' disciples had gone into town to buy some food, a Samaritan woman came to draw water from the well.

Jesus asked her, "Would you please give me a drink of water?"

[9] "You are a Jew," she replied, "and I am a Samaritan woman. How can you ask me for a drink of water when Jews and Samaritans won't have anything to do with each other?"

[10] Jesus answered, "You don't know what God wants to give you, and you don't know who is asking you for a drink. If you did, you would ask me for the water that gives life."

[11] "Sir," the woman said, "you don't even have a bucket, and the well is deep. Where are you going to get this life-giving water? [12] Our

ancestor Jacob dug this well for us, and his family and animals got water from it. Are you greater than Jacob?"

¹³ Jesus answered, "Everyone who drinks this water will get thirsty again. ¹⁴ But no one who drinks the water I give will ever be thirsty again. The water I give is like a flowing fountain that gives eternal life."

¹⁵ The woman replied, "Sir, please give me a drink of that water! Then I won't get thirsty and have to come to this well again."

¹⁶ Jesus told her, "Go and bring your husband."

¹⁷⁻¹⁸ The woman answered, "I don't have a husband."

"That's right," Jesus replied, "you're telling the truth. You don't have a husband. You have already been married five times, and the man you are now living with isn't your husband."

¹⁹ The woman said, "Sir, I can see that you are a prophet. ²⁰ My ancestors worshiped on this mountain, but you Jews say Jerusalem is the only place to worship."

²¹ Jesus said to her:

"Believe me, the time is coming when you won't worship the Father either on this mountain or in Jerusalem. ²² You Samaritans don't really know the one you worship. But we Jews do know the God we worship, and by using us, God will save the world. ²³ But a time is coming, and it is already here! Even now the true worshipers are being led by the Spirit to worship the Father according to the truth. These are the ones the Father is seeking to worship him. ²⁴ God is Spirit, and those who worship God must be led by the Spirit to worship him according to the truth."

²⁵ The woman said, "I know that the Messiah will come. He is the one we call Christ. When he comes, he will explain everything to us."

²⁶ "I am that one," Jesus told her, "and I am speaking to you now."

²⁷ The disciples returned about this time and were surprised to find Jesus talking with a woman. But none of them asked him what he wanted or why he was talking with her.

²⁸ The woman left her water jar and ran back into town. She said to the people, ²⁹ "Come and see a man who told me everything I have ever done! Could he be the Messiah?" ³⁰ Everyone in town went out to see Jesus…

⁴¹ Many more Samaritans put their faith in Jesus because of what they heard him say. ⁴² They told the woman, "We no longer have faith in Jesus just

because of what you told us. We have heard him ourselves, and we are certain that he is the Savior of the world!"

John 4.3–30, 41, 42

UNDERSTANDING THE TEXT

1. Look for all the names that Jesus is given in this passage. Do you see a progression? Look up their meanings in the glossary.

2. Try to find Samaria, Sychar, Jacob's well and Mount Gerizim on the map.

THE SAMARITAN WOMAN

LIVING TODAY

BARRIERS

Men and women build barriers between themselves that are higher and stronger than walls of concrete. But they are invisible. People accept them, and even sometimes strengthen them as if they wanted to protect themselves or as if they were afraid to be robbed or injured! From both sides of these enclosures we look at each other in anger and sometimes even raise our fists. These barriers reach everywhere — in every country and even in our minds. You know these barriers — racism, selfish wealth, religions which have become too rigid, poverty, nationalism, ideas that some people want to impose on others. When these barriers are in place, it is hard to communicate.

A SCORNED PEOPLE

Today's "Samaritans" still exist! People who are scorned because they are always struggling with economic problems, because they can't manage to develop their country, because their customs are considered primitive, different from ours, because they don't have any land on which to settle, because they are forced to ask for assistance. We don't want to interact with them, as if we think they might steal our share! People are scorned because they can't find work, because they are foreign, because they live like gypsies, or because they take drugs or are alcoholics. We don't want anything to do with them, as if we think they might ruin our good reputation.

BREAKING OUT

Jesus' Good News breaks down these barriers. It abolishes scorn! There is no one race that is better or more intelligent than another, no nation that is more religious than another. Everyone is entitled to the same abundance of God's love!

Believing in Jesus' Good News means working hard to tear down everything that separates and divides humanity. Being a Christian means destroying barriers and replacing them with respect for every person. It means practicing "astonishing" hospitality, "What you are teaching us is extraordinary! Let's put our treasures together!" It means building bridges that allow people to meet one another.

THE WELL

*Lead me, Jesus,
to the well of your Gospel,
so I can recognize you,
Lord of joy,
and offer you my faith.*

*Lead me
to the well of your Gospel
so that, near you,
I can drink the joy of knowing God
and the courage of recognizing
others as brothers and sisters.
So that I can offer them
my hospitality like a refreshing glass
of cool water under the summer sun.
So I can wash away the scorn
that people have painted
on the faces of my brothers
and sisters. So that I can welcome
gifts from the smallest
and most rejected of my brothers
and sisters that they could
never offer because
no one had ever asked them!*

*Lead me, Lord,
to the well of your Gospel,
so that I can find the living water
of the Good News.*

THE SOWER

IN JESUS' DAY

Palestinian farmers sowed their seeds on the fields before working the earth. The seeds fell in a lot of different places. The earth wasn't always good. Many seeds were lost or didn't produce fruit. In the best conditions, a field produced twenty grains for every seed planted, but usually, there were only ten.

Jesus used the example of the sower to talk about God's kingdom. He said it was like seeds thrown in a field. Some were lost. But eventually the harvest was ready. Not ten grains harvested for every seed, but thirty, even one hundred. The power of the Kingdom is greater than what we can imagine.

Those who gathered around Jesus to hear him didn't always understand what he said. They found his stories interesting but they often missed the hidden meaning, because a parable has a hidden meaning.

WHEN THE GOSPELS WERE WRITTEN

After Jesus' death and resurrection these stories were told in towns, at mealtime and during evening gatherings, by people who hadn't become Christians.

A few decades later, when Mark wrote his gospel, he included the parable of the sower. When he wrote and explained it he was thinking of his readers. They weren't country folk from Palestine, like in Jesus' day. Instead they were townspeople from Rome. They were no longer Jews but Christians. They didn't hear Jesus' voice any more but instead the Good News proclaimed by his followers. Mark called it "the message about the kingdom."

This message, like the seeds, fell on different kinds of earth. Mark's audience could discover what kind of earth they were.

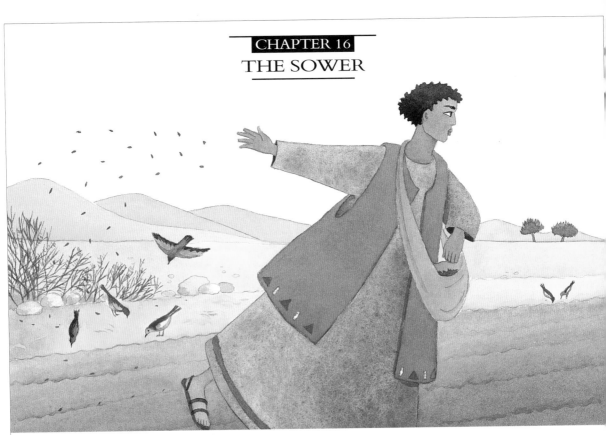

CHAPTER 16
THE SOWER

THE GOSPEL

³ "Now listen! A farmer went out to scatter seed in a field.
⁴ While the farmer was scattering the seed, some of it fell
along the road and was eaten by birds. ⁵ Other seeds fell on
thin, rocky ground and quickly started growing because the
soil wasn't very deep. ⁶ But when the sun came up, the
plants were scorched and dried up, because they did not
have enough roots. ⁷ Some also seeds fell where
thornbushes grew up and choked out the plants. So they
did not produce any grain. ⁸ But a few seeds did fall on
good ground where the plants grew and produced thirty or
sixty or even a hundred times as much as was scattered."

Then Jesus said, "If you have ears, pay attention."

³ Jesus told them:
"If you don't understand this story, you won't understand any others.
¹⁴ What the farmer is spreading is really the message about the kingdom.
¹⁵ The seeds that fell along the road are the people who hear the message. But Satan soon comes and snatches it away from them. ¹⁶ The seeds that fell on rocky ground are the people who gladly hear the message and accept it right away. ¹⁷ But they don't have any roots, and they don't last very long. As soon as life gets hard or the message gets them in trouble, they give up.

¹⁸ The seeds that fell among the thornbushes are also people who hear the message. ¹⁹ But they start worrying about the needs of this life. They are fooled by the desire to get rich and to have all kinds of other things. So the message gets choked out, and they never produce anything. ²⁰ The seeds that fell on good ground are the people who hear and welcome the message. They produce thirty or sixty or even a hundred times as much as was planted."

Mark 4.3-9, 13-20

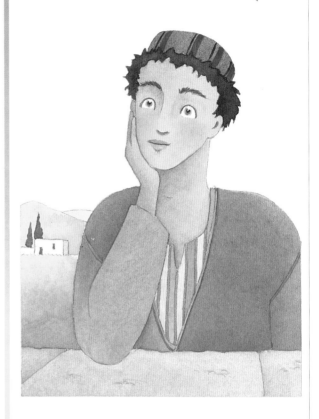

UNDERSTANDING THE TEXT

1. Begin by reading the first part (the story told in verses 3 to 9), then the second (the hidden meaning explained in verses 13 to 20).

2. Compare the four types of earth. What kinds of Christians correspond to each category?

3. Look up the meaning of the following word in the glossary: *Message* (see WORD).

LIVING
TODAY

LISTENING MEANS WELCOMING

Some people hear what is said to them. But what they hear is nothing but the sound of the wind among other noises. More noise among lots of noises. As soon as someone says something to them they forget it. Everything rolls off them, like water off a duck's back. Nothing gets through. When we talk to them it's like talking to a wall — for nothing!

Other people listen to what is said to them. They are really interested. They lend an ear and rejoice or are sad with the people who talk to them. But they don't remember for long. They pay equal attention to trivial details and to serious events. What they hear doesn't make them change their habits; they forget!

Some people welcome what they hear. They make room, as if they were opening their houses to say, "Come in, and make yourself at home!" What they hear touches them in their minds and hearts. They let themselves be disturbed, "What can I do?" What they hear transforms their lives; they begin to act.

THE WORD

Jesus Christ, the Word, is God's message for us — we hear it in everything he said. We see it in everything he did. We notice it in the hope that he raised in the Word and the meaning he gave to life. We welcome it in his Gospel. Listening to the Word means welcoming the Gospel as it is proclaimed, reflecting on it with others and praying. It also means listening to the Word in everything men and women do on earth to "sow" love for God and our neighbors. The Word is also heard in everything great and beautiful that is done.

FRUITS OF THE WORD

Very naturally all who welcome the Word of God — Jesus' message — bear fruit — they tell the truth, forgive and are forgiven, share, pray to God, distribute gifts of goodness, make room for the poor and for foreigners, offer their talents and help those who are always left behind. Wherever Christians are found, the beautiful fruit of the Word must be "harvested." The presence of the Word is not shown by good intentions or kind words; it is shown by the fruit: acts of love and justice that this Word produces.

LIVING HEARTS

Sower of living hearts,
sower of tenderness,
sower of courage,
sower of justice,
sower of prayer,
sower of light.
Lord,
sow within us!

Sower of gifts,
sower of forgiveness,
sower of faith,
sower of joy,
sower of life,
sower of the Beatitudes.
Lord, sow
in the hearts of all people!

Even if we are hard
as stones,
be patient with us!
Your Good News
will manage to slip
between the tight cracks
in our rock and will
grow into giant sheaves
of Good News!

CHAPTER 17

YEAST IN THE DOUGH

IN JESUS' DAY

During the Roman Empire people expected a period of peace and happiness. Some saw the emperor as the person who would bring them this peace and happiness. The Jews had also been waiting for a long time for a total change in society and in the world. This was their great hope. Only God could bring this about. They thought that God would come to transform everything, to re-establish justice and bring about the Kingdom. When Jesus began to talk to the crowds, he said, "The time has come! The Kingdom of God is here!" He awoke a great hope in people's hearts. The healings he performed seemed like signs of the Kingdom.

But the world wasn't transformed. The Roman occupation didn't end. Injustice continued. There was no extraordinary change. Many were disappointed: "Well, when will God's Kingdom come?" Jesus answered with two parables: "You don't see anything now. But the Kingdom is like a mustard seed. It is so small that it can hardly be seen. But it will grow into a large tree. Today we are only at the beginning. The Kingdom is hidden like yeast in dough. It can't be seen but it can make all of the dough rise. Yes, the Kingdom is there, small like a beginning. It is hidden, but it is powerful."

WHEN THE GOSPELS WERE WRITTEN

After Pentecost the early Christians kept waiting for God's Kingdom to arrive. Every day they prayed, "May your kingdom come!" But they had a long wait. Nothing extraordinary happened. However, more and more people were becoming Christians. They were like birds nesting in the branches of the mustard tree that kept growing. Could the Church be God's Kingdom?

When Matthew wrote his gospel, the world still hadn't been transformed. God still hadn't made a spectacular appearance on earth. It was understood that the Church wasn't the whole Kingdom. It was only a step, a part of the whole process. It was in the world, like yeast is in the dough. People began to understand that the Kingdom started with Jesus, that it is present now, but that it will only be fully realized at the end of time.

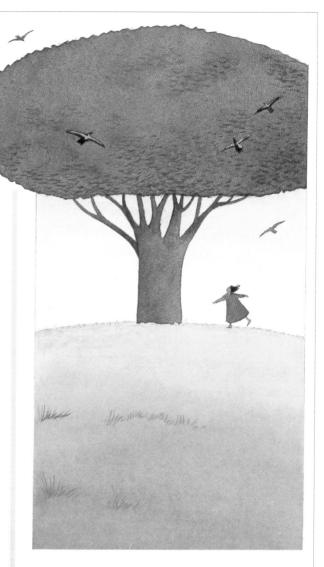

THE GOSPEL

³¹ Jesus told them another story:
"The kingdom of heaven is like what
happens when a farmer plants a mustard
seed in a field. ³² Although it is the
smallest of all seeds, it grows larger than
any garden plant and becomes a tree.
Birds even come and nest on its branches."

³³ Jesus also said:
"The kingdom of heaven is like what
happens when a woman mixes a little
yeast into three big batches of flour. Finally,
all the dough rises."

Matthew 13.31-33

UNDERSTANDING THE TEXT

1. Calculate how many ounces of yeast
are needed to make 5 loaves of bread.

2. One of the parables focuses on the power
of the Kingdom. Which parable?

3. One of the parables focuses on the humble
beginnings of the Kingdom. Which parable?

LIVING TODAY

A LARGE NUMBER

The Good News is proclaimed throughout the world and in every culture, not just to increase the number of Christians, but so the greatest number of people have the opportunity to discover Jesus Christ. In Jesus they can find joy and light for their lives. If Christians seek to be the largest group they run the risk of acting like bullies, like people who think they know it all, like "masters" who claim to be the only ones who can speak about God, like "rich" people who think they are the only ones who have the right to God's love. Being the largest group can make us want to rule over others, to dominate them, to make them think and act like us. But in fact, being the largest group requires great humility.

SMALL ACTIONS

What changes the way people act toward one another? Meetings about peace or solidarity rallies that take place once a year? What makes love grow between a man and a woman? A passionate declaration of love twice a year? And faith — a huge gathering on religious holidays? Peace grows through daily, ongoing acts of understanding and respect — by political leaders but also by individuals in their daily lives. Poverty is reduced through sharing between nations but also by efforts in towns and villages that give each and every individual a life filled with dignity and respect. Love grows through many tender words and caring gestures shared with one another throughout our lives. Faith grows through daily prayer that expresses our trust in God, and by the daily reading of God's Word. Small actions are what transforms our lives. Little by little, actions help us become better persons. Through the little actions of our daily lives, God's love, which brings about change in people and on the earth, can grow.

CHRISTIANS AS YEAST

How will the Kingdom of God, that began in Jesus, be accomplished? How does hope spread? In great bounds? Through a large number of people? God's Kingdom will be established and spread by Jesus' friends who, humbly and gently, bring as much happiness as possible to the world. Hope grows through people who, by their actions and attitude, are the yeast that make God's great love and justice increase in our society, our Church and our world.

IT'S NOTHING

It's nothing, Lord!
It's not worth mentioning.
It's simply a word
to defend the person
who was accused unfairly.
It's just money
for that person who needed it.
It's just a little patience
for another person
who has stopped searching.
It's a little consolation
for the person who is crying.
It's nothing, Lord!

It's just a prayer
in the middle of the day.
It's just a group of people
getting together to help others.
It's just forgiveness
for the person who betrayed me.
It's just a song
expressing my faith.
It's nothing, Lord!

"It's just a little bit?
It's nothing?
But it's yeast
for tomorrow's world!"
says the Lord.

JAIRUS' DAUGHTER

IN JESUS' DAY

There were many sick people. They cared for themselves as best they could. Doctors (or healers) often had poor reputations. People would say about a sick person, "She had gone to many doctors, and they had not done anything except cause her a lot of pain. She had paid them all the money she had. But instead of getting better, she only got worse" (Mark 5.26).

Many people thought that people could rise from the dead. Wasn't God master of life and death? People talked about the people miraculously raised by the prophets Elijah and Elisha eight centuries before. Sick people flocked to those who might help them. Word of Jesus' healing spread quickly among people.

Jairus, a leader in the synagogue, asked Jesus to heal his daughter who was dying. Jesus went to Jairus' house. Everyone thought the girl was already dead. Jesus took her by the hand and said to her, "Talitha, koum!" This means "Little girl, get up!" Jesus made her get up and walk again. The father better understood the meaning of his own name, "Jairus", which means "God will awaken."

Jesus didn't seek people's attention. He allowed only a few people in the girl's room with him. He told them to not tell anyone what had happened. But why? Because what Jesus had just accomplished would be understood only in the light of his own death and resurrection.

WHEN THE GOSPELS WERE WRITTEN

Mark wasn't one of those who went into the girl's room with Jesus. He learned about Jairus' daughter's awakening from Peter, who had been there. A few decades after that event, Mark wrote his gospel for people living in Rome who didn't understand Aramaic, the language Jesus spoke. That is why Mark had to translate the sentence Jesus said to the young girl, "Talitha, koum!"

For this translation, he used a Greek word which has two meanings: "wake up" and "arise" (or get up). This is the very word which the disciples and early Christians used to talk about Jesus' resurrection, "He woke up from the dead. He arose from among the dead."

With the light shed by faith in the resurrection, Mark's readers could understand what Jesus said when he saw Jairus' daughter, "She isn't dead. She is sleeping." They knew that death was only sleep from which God is able to wake us up. They knew that this power of God was in Jesus.

But there is a fundamental difference between the young girl's resurrection and Jesus' resurrection. The young girl awoke to continue her life in this world. She would die again. The resurrected Jesus is totally transformed into a new life. For Jesus there is no more death.

Christians who read Mark's story gathered strength when faced with their own death and the death of others. They knew that they would be raised by God — not for another chance at life on earth, like Jairus' daughter — but for a life without end, like Jesus at Easter.

JAIRUS' DAUGHTER

THE GOSPEL

²¹ Once again Jesus got into the boat and crossed Lake Galilee. Then as he stood on the shore, a large crowd gathered around him. ²² The person in charge of the Jewish meeting place was also there. His name was Jairus, and when he saw Jesus, he went over to him. He knelt at Jesus' feet ²³ and started begging him for help. He said, "My daughter is about to die! Please come and touch her, so she will get well and live." ²⁴ Jesus went with Jairus. Many people followed along and kept crowding around…

³⁵ While Jesus was still speaking, some men came from Jairus' home and said, "Your daughter has died! Why bother the teacher anymore?"

³⁶ Jesus heard what they said, and he said to Jairus, "Don't worry. Just have faith!"

³⁷ Jesus did not let anyone go with him except Peter and the two brothers, James and John. ³⁸ They went home with Jairus and saw the people crying and making a lot of noise. ³⁹ Then Jesus went inside and said to them, "Why are you crying and carrying on like this? The child isn't dead. She is just asleep." ⁴⁰ But the people laughed at him.

After Jesus had sent them all out of the house, he took the girl's father and mother and his three disciples and went to where she was. ⁴¹⁻⁴² He took the twelve-year-old girl by the hand and said, "Talitha, koum!" which means "Little girl, get up!" The girl got right up and started walking around.

Everyone was greatly surprised. ⁴³ But Jesus ordered them not to tell anyone what had happened. Then he said, "Give her something to eat."

Mark 5.21-24, 35-43

UNDERSTANDING THE TEXT

1. What is the attitude that the following people or groups have toward Jesus:
- the large crowd?
- Jairus?
- the people who were gathered at the house?
- those who went into the room with Jesus?

2. Which sentence shows that Jesus was seen as a healer but not as someone who could bring back life?

3. Which statement of Jesus can give you hope and strength?

LIVING TODAY

DEATH

There is a lot of pain when people we love die. It's sad to say good-bye; we can't touch them anymore, talk to them, hug them. They're gone, far from us, forever. We say, "Are they happy? Do they still love me? Will we see them again? Are they gone forever? Will they always be like this — not breathing, not talking, not laughing? Unmoving, always still?" Pain fills us and fear seizes us because death seems so final and we lose all hope. Nothing has meaning anymore. But with Jesus we can hope! He tells us, who were once afraid of death, that death is not the end. In Jesus, life follows death just as morning follows a night of sleep. Jesus gives us this new life.

DYING EVERY DAY

When we think of death we usually think of something that comes at the end of life on earth. Death comes before new life in God. But we die, a different kind of death, each day in our daily lives. We "die" when we give up in discouragement: "What good is this? I can't do anything!" When we let ourselves be overcome by despair. When we decide not to risk but let ourselves be consumed by laziness. We die when we don't act to conquer evil, when we say that the Gospel is too hard to follow and when we stop trying to live as faith-filled Christians. We die when we don't take care of anyone but ourselves, when we become self-centered. We remain frozen as if in a deep sleep, not wanting anyone to wake us up.

JESUS AWAKENS US

With Jesus we rise to new life in God. But Jesus calls us to this new life every day of our lives. He shakes us awake from every temptation, from the fear of death, from love that limits, or from empty faith. Jesus calls to us! Jesus takes us by the hand to show us God's love so we can stand alongside the poorest and smallest among us. So that we can share our food and possessions, spread our joy, and pray, filled with confidence.

HELP THEM ARISE

Lord, look at
how many children
on this earth cannot move,
and at how many have slipped
into death.

They have lost their hope,
work, their land, peace,
food and love!

Don't let this overwhelm them!
Lord, let us help them arise
from humiliation so that they may
be respected once more.
To help them arise
from loneliness so they can
speak again!
Lord, let us help them
arise from misery
so they can once again
be men and women.
To help them arise
from neglect so that they can
rejoice once more.

Lord, with your help
may we awaken our brothers
and sisters to your offer
of new life!

MULTIPLICATION OF BREAD

IN JESUS' DAY

It was spring time. The grass was green, even in Palestine. After several months in Galilee, Jesus had become well known. People came from everywhere to see him. It was impossible for Jesus to be alone. The people listened to him all day long. Evening came. It was time to eat. But how could this whole crowd be fed? There were only two solutions: buy enough food for everyone, or share what the people had brought. It would cost too much to buy bread and fish — 200 coins. (One coin represented a day's salary.)

Jesus had the disciples bring him the few loaves of bread and fish that the people had brought. He said the traditional Jewish prayer, "You are blessed, Lord, for making the earth produce bread." Then Jesus shared what was there with the whole crowd. Miraculously everyone had plenty to eat.

People were so happy that they wanted to make Jesus king. He refused; that wasn't why he had come. The symbol of the shared bread had a very different meaning.

WHEN THE GOSPELS WERE WRITTEN

The memory of this event touched the early Christians. The authors of the gospels tell about a multiplication of bread six times. Why? They want to illustrate two things:

- the importance of sharing. What matters isn't having lots of money to buy lots of things. People who buy and sell are doing business. People who share love each other. The early Christians were invited to share all they had with the poor.

- the sharing that takes place when we remember Jesus' death for us. When the early Christians got together they shared not only bread, but also remembered "the body of Christ" broken for them. The gospel accounts about the multiplication of bread state that Jesus "took the bread, raised his eyes to heaven, gave thanks, broke the bread and gave it to his disciples." The authors of the gospels wanted to show by this that sharing the bread when we gather in Church and sharing in our daily lives are closely linked.

MULTIPLICATION OF BREAD

THE GOSPEL

³⁴ When Jesus got out of the boat, he saw the large crowd that was like sheep without a shepherd. He felt sorry for the people and started teaching them many things.

³⁵ That evening the disciples came to Jesus and said, "This place is like a desert, and it is already late. ³⁶ Let the crowds leave, so they can go to the farms and villages near here and buy something to eat."

³⁷ Jesus replied, "You give them something to eat."

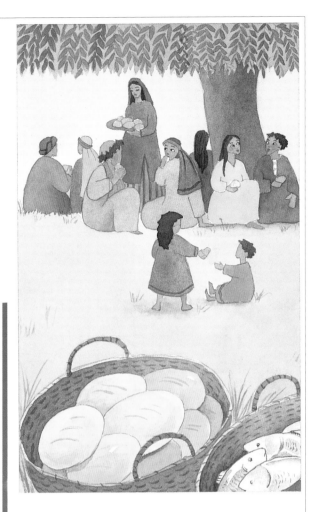

But they asked him, "Don't you know that it would take almost a year's wages to buy all of these people something to eat?" 38 Then Jesus said, "How much bread do you have? Go and see!"

They found out and answered, "We have five small loaves of bread and two fish." 39 Jesus told his disciples to have the people sit down on the green grass. 40 They sat down in groups of a hundred and groups of fifty.

41 Jesus took the five loaves and the two fish. He looked up toward heaven and blessed the food. Then he broke the bread and handed it to his disciples to give to the people. He also divided the two fish, so that everyone could have some.

42 After everyone had eaten all they wanted, 43 Jesus' disciples picked up twelve large baskets of leftover bread and fish.

44 There were five thousand men who ate the food.

Mark 6.34-44

UNDERSTANDING THE TEXT

1. Reread the passage and make two columns — one containing words that talk about *buying* and one containing words talking about *sharing*.

2. Who talks about buying and who talks about sharing?

3. What does Jesus have the disciples do to take part in sharing?

4. Why do you think the passage talks about twelve baskets?

MULTIPLICATION OF BREAD

LIVING TODAY

A WORLD OF HUNGER

For many people, each day brings only greater hunger. So much hunger and nothing to satisfy it! Some survive only because of international assistance. While much is done to help those who are hungry, it is not enough. Everyday and in every country, people go hungry. They don't have houses, salaries or jobs. To survive they have to "beg." They must depend on other people. Organizations have been created to help them. But it is not enough. How can we ever overcome famine? Why do so many people die of hunger each day? Why must whole nations be satisfied with "crumbs" while others have so much? How can you work if you are hungry? How can you love? Be happy that you are alive? Trust?

A WORLD OF SHARING

Imagine a world where buying and accumulating wealth is not important. Where it isn't important to have the most material possessions while others have less and less for themselves. Where people aren't seen as commodities that can bring profit. Imagine a world where we take care of other people's concerns and not just our own, where we share with those who have nothing so that they can regain their dignity and need to beg. A world where shared friendship is more important than the stock markets, where we help each other, where we share ideas and abilities. Where we give out of friendship and not out of our selfishness, and where everything possible is done to help others live in freedom. Famine would no longer exist! Is this a dream? No! With Jesus, this world began.

CHRISTIANS MULTIPLY BREAD

"Bread" refers to what we eat every day. But it can also refer to work, to a person's dignity, or to the opportunity to learn and receive an education. It can mean the freedom to speak, to travel freely, to believe in God and to be able to worship God openly. It can mean being able to choose the life one wants to lead. All living creatures deserve this kind of bread! Being a Christian means working toward the "multiplication" of this bread. It means taking action so that more and more people can feed themselves. Jesus gave people something to eat. Can we believe in Jesus without doing the same?

THEM

Who will help them?

*They need justice
but have no one to defend them.
They need a house
but have no one to build it.
They need land
but have nothing to plant.
They need to give
and receive love,
but have no one to love.
They need God
but have no one to tell them
about God.
They need bread
but have no one
who will share their food.
They need strength
but have no one to keep them
standing and proud.
They need music
but have no one
to teach them to sing.
They need us!
Lord, you have been with them
forever
and you call us to join them.
"Come, my friends!
We need you!"*

CHAPTER 20

PETER'S DECLARATION

IN JESUS' DAY

Many different people followed Jesus throughout Palestine. They wondered, "Who is this man? He teaches new things. He heals the sick. He spends time with everyone. He says what he thinks, even about religion." John the Baptist had been beheaded by Herod. Had John been raised up in this Jesus?

People believed that the prophet Elijah went straight to heaven without dying. Everyone expected him to return to earth. Could Elijah have returned in Jesus? God sent prophets to the Israelites in the past: Isaiah, Jeremiah, Ezekiel and many others. Could Jesus be one of these prophets? People were also waiting for a Messiah who had been chosen by God, like David. The Messiah would come to free all people. Could Jesus be this long awaited Messiah? Jesus didn't say anything. He knew that people were not ready to accept a Messiah who had to be tortured and crucified. Jesus waited for people to discover who he was, little by little.

WHEN THE GOSPELS WERE WRITTEN

After Jesus' death and resurrection the question of who he was became a bit clearer. Christians recognized in Jesus the long awaited Messiah, or Christ. They knew he wasn't the type of Messiah they had expected — a powerful king who would bring an end to the Roman occupation and restore David's former kingdom.

For many people Jesus' death on a cross remained a scandal. A crucified Messiah? Unthinkable! Mark wanted to show them that it took time to understand. Even the first of the apostles, Peter, didn't understand right away. Jesus scolded him and called him Satan.

Mark was writing for the Christians in Rome. They had just undergone a terrible persecution. Some were locked in cages with ferocious animals. Others were burned alive to light up Nero's gardens. The ones who survived had lost their friends, their parents and their possessions and nearly all hope. They found their strength in these words spoken by Jesus and recorded by Mark, "If any of you want to be my followers... you must take up your cross."

THE GOSPEL

²⁷ Jesus and his disciples went to the villages near the town of Caesarea Philippi. As they were walking along, he asked them, "What do people say about me?"

²⁸ The disciples answered, "Some say you are John the Baptist or maybe Elijah. Others say you are one of the prophets."

²⁹ Then Jesus asked them, "But who do you say I am?"

"You are the Messiah!" Peter replied.

³⁰ Jesus warned the disciples not to tell anyone about him.

³¹ Jesus began telling his disciples what would happen to him. He said, "The nation's leaders, the chief priests, and the teachers of the Law of Moses will make the Son of Man suffer terribly. He will be rejected and killed, but three days later he will rise to life." ³² Then Jesus explained clearly what he meant.

Peter took Jesus aside and told him to stop talking like that. ³³ But when Jesus turned and saw the disciples, he corrected Peter. He said to him, "Satan, get away from me! You are thinking like everyone else and not like God."

³⁴ Jesus then told the crowd and the disciples to come closer, and he said:

"If any of you want to be my followers, you must forget about yourself. You must take up your cross and follow me."

Mark 8.27-34

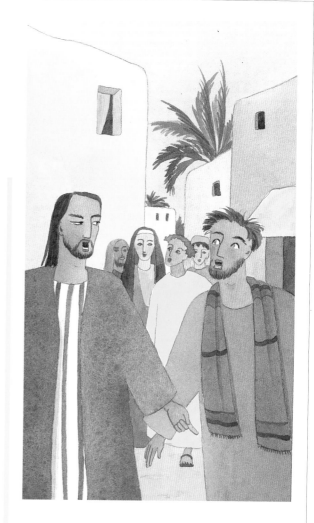

UNDERSTANDING THE TEXT

1. Look for Caesarea Philippi on the map.

2. What names are given to Jesus:
- by other people?
- by Peter?
- by Jesus himself?

3. Look up the meanings of these names in the glossary.

4. Why do you think Jesus ordered the disciples to not tell anyone that he was the Messiah?

LIVING TODAY

AND YOU?

You believe in Jesus. His word gives you life. His deeds open the way for new life. His resurrection offers hope. If someone asked you, "Who is Jesus? Tell us about him!" what would you say? That he was a special person? A great thinker with wonderful ideas? Someone who came to free humanity? The Savior? A powerful hero? The Son of God? Someone who began a religion? God sharing the lives of people? A rebel in his time? God in human form? What would you say? Who is it that you believe in?

FOLLOWING JESUS

Believing in Jesus in our daily lives doesn't mean imitating and repeating exactly what Jesus said and did when he was on earth. It means allowing ourselves to be guided by Jesus' Good News, in both the hard and beautiful moments of life. It means looking at people today with the same tenderness as Jesus. "Walking in Jesus' footsteps" doesn't mean toddling along behind him like children. It means journeying with him, sharing his trust in God and respect for others. It is hard to follow Jesus — we must make choices. Choosing one thing always means giving up something else! We can't follow Jesus' love and still behave selfishly. We can't "follow" Jesus' hospitality and still say that people are not equal. We can't "follow" Jesus' Beatitudes and not share our wealth! It is hard to follow Jesus. But if we want to follow Jesus we must be prepared to walk in his footsteps.

POWER

People admire things that are powerful, glorious and beautiful, as seen in television commercials. Crowds are drawn to people who do amazing things, who are very wealthy or who are great leaders. What a strange faith we have that honors power and external appearances! Jesus chose another path. He was often with the poor. He welcomed those who were rejected. He suffered and was put to shame on the cross — out of love. This, then, is his power — nothing stopped him from offering his life out of love!

WE BELIEVE

Lord Jesus,
we believe in you!
You were born as a baby
in our world.
You grew up as a young boy
in a family.
You worked as a man
with others in your village!
You are our Lord!
We believe in you!

Lord Jesus, we believe in you!
Arrested as a criminal,
betrayed and tortured,
rejected by your peers.
Put to death in shame,
hung on the cross,
resurrected, raised by God
from death's tomb!
You are our Lord!
We believe in you!

Lord Jesus, we believe in you!
You show us the paths
that lead to joy
by offering yourself
out of love to all the earth!
We will follow you!
We give our lives to you!

CHAPTER 21
THE TRANSFIGURATION

IN JESUS' DAY

In each person's lifetime there are moments of insight. These moments don't last very long. But now I understand a little better the answers to some important questions — Why am I alive? What is the universe? Does it have limits? Does God exist? Does God have anything to do with this world? Does God love me? What will I do in life?

Peter, James and John were the disciples who were the closest to Jesus. One day they had an experience. Jesus took them to the top of a high mountain, likely Mount Tabor, that was about 1800 feet high. There they discovered two other people who had gone alone to a mountaintop during their lifetime, and who, according to the Bible, met God: Moses in fire, light, clouds and the storm; Elijah in the silence of a light breeze. There they were, talking with Jesus.

Peter, James and John had been with Jesus for quite a while. They already understood that God was close to them. Now, alone on the mountain, they discovered the relationship among Moses, Elijah and Jesus. They also understood that, of the three, Jesus was closest to God and closest to them. For a brief moment, they saw who Jesus really was. It was like a bright light. Jesus was transformed, transfigured. The three disciples wanted to remain in the security of this discovery. But they realized very quickly that they were still standing on solid ground. As they came down from the mountain they wondered where this experience would lead them.

WHEN THE GOSPELS WERE WRITTEN

Mark, who tells us the story of the transfiguration, wasn't on the mountain. But his friend Peter certainly told him about it. When Mark wrote his gospel he knew that Jesus had been crucified and he believed in his resurrection. He believed that Jesus was not only the long-awaited Messiah, but also the beloved Son of God. This truth wasn't easy to discover and to accept; it was even harder to understand. God's help was needed.

Mark shows that it is God who helps us understand who Jesus is. As at Jesus' baptism, a mysterious voice was heard, "This is my Son, and I love him. Listen to what he says."

At times the early Christians were tempted to look for extraordinary things, great revelations or ecstasy in order to have faith. This is like trying to escape from the world and "get high" on religion. Mark brings the disciples (and us) back to reality. The transfiguration only lasted a brief moment. And Peter didn't know what he was saying when he asked to remain there. He was bewildered.

CHAPTER 21
THE TRANSFIGURATION

THE GOSPEL

2 Six days later Jesus took Peter, James, and John with him. They went up on a high mountain, where they could be alone. There in front of the disciples, Jesus was completely changed. 3 And his clothes became much whiter than any bleach on earth could make them. 4 Then Moses and Elijah were there talking with Jesus.

^{5} Peter said to Jesus, "Teacher, it is good for us to be here! Let us make three shelters, one for you, one for Moses, and one for Elijah." ^{6} But Peter and the others were terribly frightened, and he did not know what he was talking about.

^{7} The shadow of a cloud passed over and covered them. From the cloud a voice said, "This is my Son, and I love him. Listen to what he says!" ^{8} At once the disciples looked around, but they saw only Jesus.

^{9} As Jesus and his disciples were coming down the mountain, he told them not to say a word about what they had seen, until the Son of Man had been raised from death. ^{10} So they kept it to themselves. But they wondered what he meant by the words "raised from death."

Mark 9.2-10

UNDERSTANDING THE TEXT

1. Look for Mount Tabor on the map.

2. What is the imagery expressed in "cloud"? Look up the word in the glossary.

3. Make a list of the characters in the story. There are seven of them. Be careful because one of them is not named. Why not?

4. Make the following diagram. Write "Jesus" in the middle. Write the names of the characters in the story around his name. Draw a different colored line from the characters to Jesus according to the relationship they had with him.

5. Where would you include your name on this diagram?

THE TRANSFIGURATION

LIVING TODAY

QUESTIONS

We spend most of our lives searching for the direction we should take – "Is thi really what I should do?" We ask questions about ourselves and others – "Where do belong? What occupation should I choose? What are my talents? How can I love? Ho can I share?" We ask questions about the world – "How can we all work together? Ho can I fight evil? How can we all get along?" We ask questions about God – "Where can meet God? Is God interested in human beings? Does God really exist? How can believe in God?" We ask questions throughout our lifetime. Sometimes we feel that w can't see our way clearly.

TIMES OF REVELATION

Sometimes it feels as if the fog of all these questions lifts for an instant and we ca see clearly! For a very short time the answers become clear as daylight! We see whicl path to follow, what we can do, what work is needed to change the world and how Go calls us. At these times our love and faith in God is strong. These are moments of trans figuration, when we can see beyond our everyday reality. We discover light, "It's clear Now I really understand." These moments are as fleeting and fragile as a ray of sunshine Afterward everything returns to normal. But we carry this discovery within us. We sav with new eyes and we have the strength to continue trying to love and believe, one da at a time. These moments can come in prayer or reflection, during a discussion, whe we share, or through other people.

MORE THAN SKIN DEEP

Often we are so happy that we could burst! When we love and are loved in retur we could dance on rooftops! When we discover God's deepest love we want to shout i to the whole world! It can be seen on our faces; our faces are transformed. We are fille with light, joy, love and faith in God. We can see beyond our everyday truths; our hearts secrets are burning on our faces! Our faces are transformed and made beautiful b God's love!

IT IS EASY
TO SEE

It is easy to see, Lord Jesus.
In you we see
God's face
leaning close to earth
and whispering,
"You are my children!
Don't ever be afraid!
I will always be with you!"

Where should we turn,
Lord Jesus, to see
God's face in our world today?
Where people pray
with their whole hearts?
Where people share
with open arms?
Where people love
with their whole lives?
Where people sing
with loud voices?
Where forgiveness of sins
is given freely?
Show us, Lord,
the face of God
that shines
in our world today.

CHAPTER 22
THE GOOD SAMARITAN

IN JESUS' DAY

Many scholars, teachers of the Law and chief priests didn't like Jesus. They were angry with Jesus because he upset them. He asked questions that embarrassed and trapped them. Jesus didn't let them get away with anything. He understood their game.

Someone asked Jesus, "What should I do to have eternal life?" "You know very well," Jesus said. "You know the Law. Just like every practicing Jew, you recite this passage twice a day, 'You will love the Lord your God with all your heart, soul and strength.'"

Another question was, "Then who is this neighbor that I have to love?" Jesus told them a story. A man was in the desert and was attacked by criminals. He was left for dead. Three men walked by: a priest of the Temple, a Levite (someone who served in the Temple) and a Samaritan (a foreigner who was not well liked in Israel). Which of the three treated the wounded man like his neighbor? Not the one you might think.

WHEN THE GOSPELS WERE WRITTEN

The story of this man who was attacked by thieves is found only in Luke's gospel. Luke isn't addressing — like Jesus was — teachers of the Law, but Christians from different countries. Some were from Jewish origins. Others had been non-Jews.

Luke wants to make them understand:

- that Jesus continued to teach things that were found in Jewish Law (in the Hebrew Scriptures): "Love God and your neighbor!"

- that he broadened this teaching. Now your neighbor isn't only the person who lives near you or in the same country; but your neighbor is every human being.

- that the Samaritan (the foreigner) is closer to God than the priest and the Levite.

It doesn't matter where we come from. What counts is what we do for our neighbor.

CHAPTER 22
THE GOOD SAMARITAN

THE GOSPEL

^{25} An expert in the Law of Moses stood up and asked Jesus a question to see what he would say. "Teacher," he asked, "what must I do to have eternal life?"

^{26} Jesus answered, "What is written in the Scriptures? How do you understand them?"

^{27} The man replied, "The Scriptures say, 'Love the Lord your God with all your heart, soul, strength, and mind.' They also say, 'Love your neighbors as much as you love yourself.'"

^{28} Jesus said, "You have given the right answer. If you do this, you will have eternal life."

^{29} But the man wanted to show that he knew what he was talking about. So he asked Jesus, "Who are my neighbors?"

³⁰ Jesus replied:

As a man was going down from Jerusalem to Jericho, robbers attacked him and grabbed everything he had. They beat him up and ran off, leaving him half dead.

³¹ A priest happened to be going down the same road. But when he saw the man, he walked by on the other side. ³² Later a temple helper came to the same place. But when he saw the man who had been beaten up, he also went by on the other side.

³³ A man from Samaria then came traveling along that road. When he saw the man, he felt sorry for him ³⁴ and went over to him. He treated his wounds with olive oil and wine and bandaged them. Then he put him on his own donkey and took him to an inn, where he took care of him. ³⁵ The next morning he gave the innkeeper two silver coins and said, "Please take care of the man. If you spend more than this on him, I will pay you when I return."

³⁶ Then Jesus asked, "Which one of these three people was a real neighbor to the man who was beaten up by robbers?"

³⁷ The teacher answered, "The one who showed pity."

Jesus said, "Go and do the same!"

Luke 10.25-37

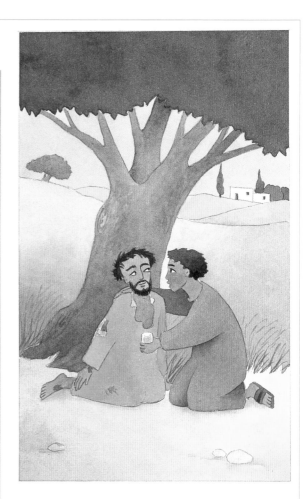

UNDERSTANDING THE TEXT

1. Look on the map and find the route from Jerusalem to Jericho.

2. Look up the following words in the glossary: *Law, Levite (temple helper)* and *Samaritan.*

3. Can you think of another time in Jesus' life when he had something to do with Samaria? (See Chapter 15.)

4. Make three columns — one each for the priest, the Levite (temple helper) and the Samaritan. Write what each person did for the wounded man. Compare the columns.

THE GOOD SAMARITAN

NEIGHBORS

The word *neighbor* can mean a lot. My neighbors are close by, though I may not notice them since I am so accustomed to their presence. They are part of my daily life; we see one another every day. Whether they are near or far, my neighbor is the person who turns to me, and to whom I turn, for help or for a listening ear. We support one another. A person in need is always my neighbor, and when I help someone, I am the neighbor of that person. We are part of the same human family. Every human being, without exception, is my neighbor.

DRAWING NEARER

At times we withdraw from our neighbors. Why? Perhaps we're afraid of the commitment we might have to make. But we know that there is only one way to treat another human being — to offer help when help is needed. To be as close as possible so our neighbor can see us and not feel alone. To help him or her get up with dignity. We are good neighbors when we reach out to people who have been left lying alone in their misery.

SAMARITANS

Today's "good Samaritans" are well known. They can be found wherever people need help: Where people lack friendship or shelter or where they are rejected because they are different; where people's voices have been silenced, and where they have lost their rights. Good Samaritans give all that they can — their time, resources and love. They hold nothing back. They are not selective. They go to everyone, without exception. For them each person in need is a human being crying for help. Good Samaritans have only one concern: to help immediately and freely, to the best of their abilities. All Christians are called to be "good Samaritans," the neighbors of everyone in need.

ALONG THE ROAD

*Lord, you call us
to be Good Samaritans.
You call us
to serve the world
following your Good News plan.
We find joy
in being able to help
our brothers and sisters!
Lord, we are your friends.
We want to walk with you
along your path of life.*

*Good Samaritans welcome those
who are rejected.
Good Samaritans
talk to and respect those
who have been isolated.
Good Samaritans bring hope
to those who have failed,
and they reach out to those
who are ridiculed!
Good Samaritans see the stranger
as a brother or a sister.
O Lord, give us the strength
of Good Samaritans
as we walk your path of life.*

THE PRODIGAL SON

IN JESUS' DAY

Jesus didn't see distinctions between people. He welcomed everyone — people who were "OK" and those who weren't. Tax collectors, for example, weren't very well liked. A Samaritan woman belonged to a group that was despised. Wasn't a Roman soldier a foreigner and a pagan? These people were all seen as sinners, as impure and unworthy of God's love. But not in Jesus' eyes.

Rumors about Jesus were flying. Scribes and Pharisees criticized him openly, "It's OK if he hangs around people who obey the Law, like us. But it's scandalous when he welcomes people of bad reputation and sinners and eats with them. That just isn't done."

Jesus defended his position by telling several stories. A lamb wandered away from the flock. The shepherd looked for it. The shepherd was very happy when he found it. A woman lost a coin. She looked for it everywhere. She rejoiced with her friends when she found it. A man watched his son leave home. The father rejoiced and organized a celebration to welcome the son when he returned home.

Each one of these stories, or parables, has the same message: we are happy when we find something that had been lost. It is the same with God. God rejoices at the return of people who once turned away. God does everything to welcome them. This is what Jesus does when he welcomes publicans and sinners.

WHEN THE GOSPELS WERE WRITTEN

Luke hadn't known Jesus when he was alive. Therefore Luke hadn't heard Jesus telling the parables. But the early Christians kept Jesus' teachings alive through their storytelling. Luke must have heard the story of the father who watches his ungrateful son leave and who later welcomes him joyfully when he returns home.

Luke wasn't addressing the inhabitants of Palestine, as Jesus had. Luke had traveled a lot and knew Christians in many towns in the Roman Empire. Among them there were rich and poor, converts from Judaism and from paganism, people who were thought to be righteous and others who were seen as sinners.

There were also people who thought they were better than others. They were like the Pharisees who bragged about obeying the Law. They were also like the older son in the parable. He didn't leave his father. He was proud to say, "I never disobeyed any of your orders!"

Luke specifically wanted to show these people how strong God's love is for the sinner who returns home — similar to the father who runs to meet his ungrateful son.

Luke didn't give an ending to the story. Will the older brother remain angry? Or will he rejoice with his brother and father? The question isn't answered. Luke's readers must answer this question through the way they live.

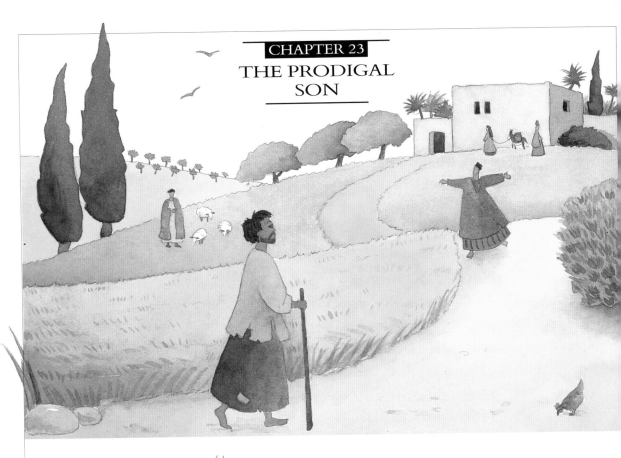

THE PRODIGAL SON

THE GOSPEL

¹¹ Jesus also told them another story:

Once a man had two sons. ¹² The younger son said to his father, "Give me my share of the property." So the father divided his property between his two sons.

¹³ Not long after that, the younger son packed up everything he owned and left for a foreign country, where he wasted all his money in wild living. ¹⁴ He had spent everything, when a bad famine spread through that whole land. Soon he had nothing to eat.

¹⁵ He went to work for a man in that country, and the man sent him out to take care of his pigs. ¹⁶ He would have been glad to eat what the pigs were eating, but no one gave him a thing.

¹⁷ Finally, he came to his senses and said, "My father's workers have plenty to eat, and here I am, starving to death! ¹⁸ I will go to my father and say to him, 'Father, I have sinned against God in heaven and against you. ¹⁹ I am no longer good enough to be called your

son. Treat me like one of your workers.' "

²⁰ The younger son got up and started back to his father. But when he was still a long way off, his father saw him and felt sorry for him. He ran to his son and hugged and kissed him.

²¹ The son said, "Father, I have sinned against God in heaven and against you. I am no longer good enough to be called your son."

²² But his father said to the servants, "Hurry and bring the best clothes and put them on him. Give him a ring for his finger and sandals for his feet. ²³ Get the best calf and prepare it, so we can eat and celebrate. ²⁴ This son of mine was dead, but has now come back to life. He was lost and has now been found." And they began to celebrate.

²⁵ The older son had been out in the field. But when he came near the house, he heard the music and dancing. ²⁶ So he called one of the servants over and asked, "What's going on here?"

²⁷ The servant answered, "Your brother has come home safe and sound, and your father ordered us to kill the best calf." ²⁸ The older brother got so angry that he would not even go into the house.

His father came out and begged him to go in. ²⁹ But he said to his father, "For years I have worked for you like a slave and have always obeyed you. But you have never even given me a little goat, so that I could give a dinner for my friends. ³⁰ This other son of yours wasted your money on prostitutes. And now that he has come home, you ordered the best calf to be killed for a feast."

³¹ His father replied, "My son, you are always with me, and everything I have is yours. ³² But we should be glad and celebrate! Your brother was dead, but he is now alive. He was lost and has now been found."

Luke 15.11-32

UNDERSTANDING THE TEXT

1. Look for all the words and expressions that show the love that the father has for his son.

2. Imagine one (or two) endings to this parable. What will the older son do?

3. What title would you give this passage?

LIVING TODAY

Better

We accuse other people of being liars, of not being true to their word, of acting like bad Christians, or of... Why? Perhaps so we won't see our sin, or so we can say, "At least our hands are clean. We're not like them! We don't do anything wrong. Our words are good and our thoughts are clean! We're always on God's side! We are from the true Church!" We think that we are better than "those poor sinners." We deny our own sinfulness when we think that we are better than others, or when we think our rights are more important than others. God has a lovely spot reserved for us in heaven; God smiles at us more dearly, and God has great things in store for us — right? God must certainly see our righteousness; aren't we more faithful than the others? Where does this pride that fills our hearts originate?

Coming back

Sin consists of turning away from God, of turning our backs on God. Of withdrawing as if to say, "I'll find better things somewhere else. It's too restrictive near you. I don't have enough space to organize my life the way I want. You keep me from doing what I want, and I don't need you!"

Conversion consists in turning back to God, in turning our lives toward God, in drawing nearer as if to say, "I cannot live away from you. I am happy when I am near you. The source of my happiness is in your presence and your Word. Help me to be free and to grow."

God's open arms

God does not have favorites. Whether we are good or sinful, God wants us to be close to him and he loves us. Those who leave are always welcomed back. God waits patiently for those who go astray to come back. God even goes to them to lessen the space that separates them, to be closer to them. God doesn't turn away from anyone; God looks at us with love and with open arms. There is no punishment waiting for those who return from far away; instead a celebration of love awaits them!

TENDERNESS

Others tell us,
"You are nothing. You are sinful
and we are ashamed of you
because of your sinful life."
But God,
you accept us as we are.
You cleanse us
with your tenderness.

Others tell us,
"We won't have anything to do
with you. You don't belong here
any more. You don't think
or act like us.
You didn't respect our law."
But God,
you open your arms to us
and our spoiled lives
and you surround us
with tenderness.

Others tell us,
"There's no room here for traitors.
There is no respect here
for those who ran away.
There are no rights here
for deserters."
But God,
you hold us tight in your arms
and show us
your great tenderness!

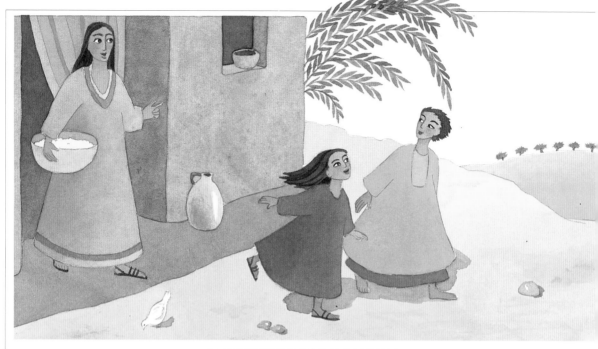

CHAPTER 24
JESUS AND THE CHILDREN

IN JESUS' DAY

In Jesus' day parents hoped to have a large family. They considered children to be blessings from God. Children listened to, obeyed and respected their parents. Children were entirely dependent on their parents. If children didn't obey, a suitable punishment soon reminded them how to behave.

Parents were often concerned about the future of their children. When they met someone famous, like a rabbi or a priest, they asked him to touch the child as a blessing. This physical contact was like a promise for a good future.

Since parents knew that Jesus was an extraordinary person, they often brought their babies or children to him to be touched. But the disciples would chase them away because they were worried about keeping order. They thought that Jesus had better things to do than worry about children.

Jesus got angry. (He didn't get angry often.) He said that the children must be allowed to come to him. He kissed them and blessed them. He used them as an example — to enter God's kingdom, you have be like the children.

WHEN THE GOSPELS WERE WRITTEN

Like Matthew and Luke, Mark also included the story of Jesus and the children. But Mark is the only one to mention that Jesus got angry and that he blessed the children. Peter, one of the disciples, probably gave this extra information to Mark. But why did Mark decide to include this story?

Mark was writing for Christians who met regularly. Children of all ages were present at these meetings. At times they were a nuisance. Mark wanted to show people that they should accept the children as Jesus did. Mark was writing for people who thought it was complicated to get into God's kingdom, or to be a Christian. Mark told them, "All you have to do is be like a little child."

Mark was writing for Christians who argued sometimes about who should be the leader of the group. Who is in charge? Who is most important? Mark told them, "You should ask instead: who is most like a child?"

Mark was writing for Christians whose leaders received their power from the laying on of hands. They should be like those children on whom Jesus laid his hands.

THE GOSPEL

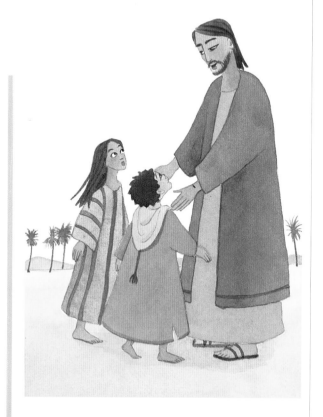

¹³ Some people brought their children to Jesus so that he could bless them by placing his hands on them. But his disciples told the people to stop bothering him.

¹⁴ When Jesus saw this, he became angry and said, "Let the children come to me! Don't try to stop them. People who are like these little children belong to the kingdom of God. ¹⁵ I promise you that you cannot get into God's kingdom, unless you accept it the way a child does." ¹⁶ Then Jesus took the children in his arms and blessed them by placing his hands on them.

Mark 10.13-16

UNDERSTANDING THE TEXT

1. Who are the characters in the story and what do they do?

2. What do the parents want who bring their children to Jesus (v. 13)? What did they receive (v. 16)? Compare the two things. What do you think about this comparison?

3. Look up the meanings of the following words in the glossary: *disciples, laying on hands,* and *the Kingdom of God.*

LIVING
TODAY

THE WORLD'S CHILDREN

There are millions of happy children in the world. But there are many, many more children who are suffering. Children who have lost their parents, who are beaten, who are dying from hunger and cold, or who live in shelters made from cloth and cardboard. Children who live in refugee camps. Children who must search through the garbage in order to find something to eat. Children who beg. Children caught in wars where they are surrounded by weapons that bring about death. Children who are forced to work as slaves. Children who grow up surrounded by violence, who give their lives over to drugs, who can't go to school or learn because they are too poor. Children of joy and suffering represent the world's future and its happiness! They are God's beloved children.

"LET THE CHILDREN COME!"

We hear a very clear message when Jesus says, "Don't stop the children!" We must protect children as we protect all of human life. Each child is an individual who is learning to think, to make decisions, to love, to know God and to respect others. It is so important to ensure that, in their families and societies, children can grow and develop, find their place, make the world more human, discover God, and be free to follow, if they choose, the path of faith.

The United Nations and many other organizations work to protect the rights of children. Their documents echo Jesus' loud call to let the children be.

We can't be faithful to Jesus' teaching if we don't bring food, love, comfort, education, awareness and dignity to all human beings and above all to children.

BEING LIKE CHILDREN

Jesus tells us that we must be like children in order to welcome the gospel and live according to his Word. Obviously this doesn't mean being childish or acting like a baby. Like the little children, Jesus' friends are not proud; they are not certain that they know everything about life. They need others; they need their love. They need God and God's Word. They have lots to learn. They don't claim to know everything or to possess the truth. They don't think that they are the strongest. They hesitate. They accept being taught, learning continuously. They rejoice in the world's happiness and protest against evil. They pursue happiness and encourage others to join them in their dance. They throw themselves wholeheartedly into the work of proclaiming the Gospel joyously.

INSTRUCTION

You want me, Lord,
to be a child of the gospel?

I, who like to be in charge, Lord,
and make others do what I want?
I, who like to be the strongest?
to be right? to talk first
and not listen to others?
I, who have temper tantrums
to get my way?
Me, Lord?

Teach me, Lord,
so I can become a child
of the gospel!
Teach me your commandment
so I may love God
and serve my neighbor.
Teach me to be attentive
to your life-changing Word!
Teach me to let go
of my pride and my lies.
Teach my spirit so that
I can look for you and follow you
with my whole heart.

Oh Lord, how I would love
to become a child of the Gospel!

CHAPTER 25
THE RICH YOUNG MAN

IN JESUS' DAY

Many people followed Jesus. Some left everything just to be with him. Peter, Andrew and John left their father and his small fishing business. Levi (also called Matthew) quit his job as a tax collector. Others left their homes, their families and their towns. Some were poor. They didn't have any possessions, a job or even a family. They were freer to follow Jesus. Jesus preached the Kingdom, a new life. The Kingdom had begun and would last forever. It would conquer death. Jesus called it "eternal life."

A young man ran to Jesus, full of good intentions. "What do I have to do to have eternal life?" He already obeyed all of the commandments. Jesus suggested that he do much more: "Sell your possessions and give the money to the poor!" The young man lowered his head and went away very sad. He was too rich. He didn't have the strength to give up his possessions. Jesus didn't hold him back. Jesus doesn't force anyone to follow him.

WHEN THE GOSPELS WERE WRITTEN

Mark told this story to the Christians in his community. There were both rich and poor people. Mark was addressing mainly the rich. What was he trying to say?

- that Jesus loved them just as he loved the young man who ran to him;

- that Jesus asked them to obey the commandments. But Mark added one more to his list, "Do not cheat." This means, for those who had servants, slaves or employees, "You will pay them enough, and on time." The apostle James used this same expression "refuse to pay" to scold the rich: "You refused to pay the people who worked in your fields…" (James 5.4).

- that Jesus suggested one more step. Some Christians already sold what they had and shared the money with the poor (Acts 2.44, 45). Why won't you do the same? The joy of sharing is worth more than the misery of selfishness.

THE GOSPEL

¹⁷ As Jesus was walking down a road, a man ran up to him. He knelt down, and asked, "Good teacher, what can I do to have eternal life?"

¹⁸ Jesus replied, "Why do you call me good? Only God is good. ¹⁹ You know the commandments.'Do not murder. Be faithful in marriage. Do not steal. Do not tell lies about others. Do not cheat. Respect your father and mother.'"

²⁰ The man answered, "Teacher, I have obeyed all these commandments since I was a young man."

²¹ Jesus looked closely at the man. He liked him and said, "There's one thing you still need to do. Go sell everything you own. Give the money to the poor, and you will have riches in heaven. Then come with me."

²² When the man heard Jesus say this, he went away gloomy and sad because he was very rich.

Mark 10.17-22

UNDERSTANDING THE TEXT

1. What had the young man done before he met Jesus? What more did Jesus ask of him?

2. Of all Jesus' actions or attitudes, which one seems to be the most important?

3. Compare verses 17 and 22. Choose from the following list of words the ones that match the verses: arrival, departure; sadness, joy; openness, withdrawal; past, future; meeting, separation.

4. Look up the meaning of the word *rich* in the glossary.

LIVING
TODAY

Rich

People are considered rich when they have lots of possessions. When they can buy anything they want without worrying how much it costs. When they don't have to worry about saving for tomorrow.

We are rich when we have friends. When we can have an education. When we have time for our hobbies or leisure activities. When we can rely on our friends. When we have abilities and strengths. When we are loved. There are different ways of being rich! Being rich isn't a sin. It's good, but it's also a responsibility.

In Chains

Jesus doesn't condemn the rich. He only cautions them against becoming slaves to their possessions. If they aren't careful, what they own will control their thoughts and their actions. If they aren't careful their lives will begin to revolve around what they own. Everything else will lose importance — people, God, loving and sharing with others. Some rich people want to have their cake and eat it, too. Their only happiness is in owning things; they are chained to their riches. They only want to "have"; they value their possessions more than relationships with people and with God.

Following Jesus

We can't journey with Jesus if we have too many burdens or if we are always looking back, regretfully, at what we left behind. We can't love if all we think about is what we own. Because, when we love, we share what we have and who we are. With Jesus Christ we grow and develop. Living by half measures no longer satisfies us. We give all we can. We don't hold back; we give it all as Jesus did throughout his whole life. The more we have, the more we are called to share!

Free

We can accept or refuse to follow Jesus. We are all free — in our hearts and in our lives. Christ offers his love to us no matter what we decide. What counts is that we start to walk with Jesus. Perhaps one day his call will touch our hearts and help us understand that we are able to go much further.

RICH

*If you are rich
with love,
happiness,
joy and faith,
what treasures you possess!
Come and give!*

*If you are rich with friends,
welcome others!
If you are rich with laughter,
console others!
If you are rich with prayer,
pray for your brothers and sisters!
What treasures you possess!
Give without measure!*

*You who know how to speak,
come to the defense of those
who have been silenced.
You who are strong,
encourage those who falter
and support those who stagger
under the heavy burden of life.
You who are surrounded
with happiness,
share your light with those
who are alone and fearful.
What treasures you possess!
You have received so much.
All I ask is that you share
what you have received!*

CHAPTER 26

BARTIMAEUS, THE BLIND MAN

IN JESUS' DAY

The town of Jericho is about 22 miles from Jerusalem. It is a quiet little town near the Dead Sea, a peaceful oasis in the middle of the desert. Herod renovated the town as a winter residence for influential people from Jerusalem. There was a large supply of water there, due to a system of springs and aqueducts. This is why it was called "the city of palm trees." Jericho was also a place where pilgrims stopped on their way to Jerusalem, a day's walk away.

There were many beggars outside the city gates who held out their hands to every passerby. They were people who had been rejected by society. They didn't have any income and were often sick and without help. In Jesus' day there was no Social Security. Among the beggars was Bartimaeus, a blind man. That day, like every day, he hoped to get a few coins. But that day would be different from all the others. Bartimaeus, the blind man, wasn't deaf. He heard that Jesus and his disciples were going to pass his way. Like the rest of the Jewish people, he was waiting for the Messiah to free and save them. Perhaps he would even be healed. There they were — Bartimaeus cried out as loudly as he could. He called Jesus by the name that was reserved for the Messiah, "Son of David!" Jesus heard him. Jesus healed and restored his sight, and Bartimaeus followed Jesus. Jesus had opened his eyes, but there was so much more to discover!

WHEN THE GOSPELS WERE WRITTEN

Mark wrote about the healing of the blind man specifically for Christians who sometimes had a hard time seeing who Jesus was and understanding him. Like Bartimaeus they needed to be healed and saved. Like him they understood fairly easily that Jesus was the "Son of David." But Jesus was so much more than that.

There were many things left for them to discover. Why was Jesus crucified? What does it mean when we say, "He is risen?"

Like the blind man, they use the same words, "Take pity on me" or "Take pity on us." The Christians didn't pray at the gates of Jericho. They gathered in their houses to pray and to remember Jesus.

Matthew and Luke also tell of this healing. But they don't give the name of the blind man. Why does Mark call him "Bartimaeus, the son of Timaeus"? Perhaps it's because this man, who became a Christian, was well known by the people who read Mark's gospel.

THE GOSPEL

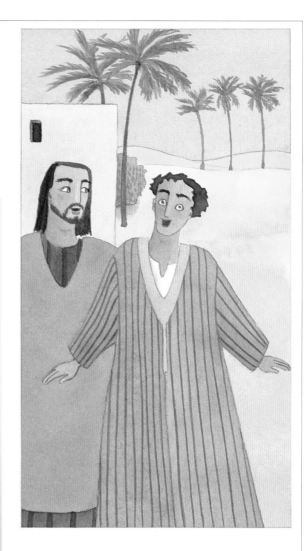

⁴⁶ Jesus and his disciples went to Jericho. And as they were leaving, they were followed by a large crowd. A blind beggar by the name of Bartimaeus son of Timaeus was sitting beside the road. ⁴⁷ When he heard that it was Jesus from Nazareth, he shouted, "Jesus, Son of David, have pity on me!" ⁴⁸ Many people told the man to stop, but he shouted even louder, "Son of David, have pity on me!"

⁴⁹ Jesus stopped and said, "Call him over!"

They called out to the blind man and said, "Don't be afraid! Come on! He is calling for you." ⁵⁰ The man threw off his coat as he jumped up and ran to Jesus.

⁵¹ Jesus asked, "What do you want me to do for you?"

The blind man answered, "Master, I want to see!"

⁵² Jesus told him, "You may go. Your eyes are healed because of your faith."

Right away the man could see, and he went down the road with Jesus.

Mark 10.46-52

UNDERSTANDING THE TEXT

1. Reread the passage and make three columns — one for what Jesus does, one for what the blind man does and one for what the others do.

2. What changed for the blind man? Was it only his sight that he found?

3. Locate Jericho on the map and trace the route from Jericho to Jerusalem.

4. Look up the meanings of the following words in the glossary: *Son of David* and *rabbi (master)*.

CHAPTER 26
BARTIMAEUS,
THE BLIND MAN

Beggars

When we don't have enough food or when we are unhappy, we reach a poin
where we sit back and plead for help. Life and happiness depend on it. Begging is askin
for what is necessary to live as human beings. In one way or another, we are all beggar
We beg for dignity when we have lost our rights. We beg for justice when we are perse
cuted. We beg for respect when no one listens to us. We beg for friendship when w
have been abandoned and yearn to love and be loved. We beg for food when we suffe
from hunger. We beg for sympathy when life's burdens are too hard to carry. We beg fo
healing when we can't bear the suffering any longer. We beg for forgiveness when w
want to be freed from the sin that holds us captive. We beg for faith when we want to b
sure of God. To whom can we turn?

The blind

Jesus listens to our begging! Jesus reaches out to grab our outstretched hands t
save us and to free us from all that oppresses us, and to lead us on the path of life. Bu
often our spirits and hearts remain blinded. We refuse to see him! "What good is cryin
out to him? Maybe we are better off placing our hope in riches and pleasure: Is it wort
trusting Jesus? Does he really take care of all who cry for help?" We lose faith and clos
our hearts to his Word of Good News. We don't see the signs of his love around us: a
that people do in his name to help their brothers and sisters! We close our minds; w
don't try to get to know Jesus.

Opening our eyes

Believing in Jesus the Christ is like opening our eyes — we recognize that h
alone heals and saves us. That he alone tears us away from the things that keep us fro
living. When we cry out he answers us by showing us God's tenderness, by inviting us t
share our bread and joy with others, by freeing us from the chains of sin, by offering u
his presence, by offering us new life after death. Jesus heals and saves us by inviting us t
live with him!

OPEN

Take pity on me, Lord!
I am small
and can't do anything
with this sin
that holds me captive,
that makes me repeat
the same mistakes
and fall into the same temptations.
O Christ, Son of God,
give me trust!

So many questions
fill my heart.
Why do nations choose war
before peace?
Why must suffering
destroy happiness?
Why does death
come and take away life?
Why are innocent people
so often hurt?
O Christ, Son of God,
give me hope!

Give me faith,
O Christ, Son of God,
so that I can see in you
the Savior of the living,
the Lord who triumphs over death!

THE ENTRY INTO JERUSALEM

IN JESUS' DAY

One day Jesus said, "We are going to Jerusalem." His friends were concerned. They were fearful. In the countryside they were free to do and say what they wanted. In Jerusalem, the capital, they would have to answer to the chief priests. And Jesus had already mentioned that this might not be so easy. But they believed in their master. They followed him.

The great Jewish holiday of Passover was near. Pilgrims from everywhere, not only from Palestine but from throughout the Roman Empire, were making their way toward Jerusalem. Jesus and his friends approached the town. Jesus was well known. Some Galileans had arrived in Jerusalem before him. People acclaimed Jesus as king and Messiah. Many cried out "Hosanna!" which meant "Save us!" — we might say, "Hooray for God!" They dreamed of a new kingdom, like David's — where the people would be free, independent and happy. They dreamed that Jesus would accomplish this.

Jesus didn't refuse the title of Messiah or Son of David. But he showed that the role of the Messiah was not what everyone thought. The mount of a king, a warrior and a conqueror was a horse. Jesus didn't ride a horse. He entered Jerusalem on the back of a donkey. This was the mount of a poor man, a common man, and of a Messiah who refused the trappings of a king. Jesus hadn't come to overthrow the Romans. What he came to do was much more important.

All of this happened on the first day of the week (our Sunday). The days that followed would be difficult. The disciples were right to be afraid.

WHEN THE GOSPELS WERE WRITTEN

In the year 30 A.D., when people were crying out "Hooray for God" as Jesus entered Jerusalem, no one knew the outcome of the week that was just beginning. The authors of the gospel, writing much later, knew that on the Friday of the same week Jesus would be put to death.

Toward the end of the first century the Romans were still in power, stronger than ever. The early Christians had had time to understand that the result of the Gospel was more than a futile war against Rome.

When Mark wrote his gospel, he was writing first of all to Christians who lived in Rome. These people lived in situations similar to what Jesus experienced in Jerusalem. Jesus' story became, in some ways, their story.
- Like Jesus they were in a capital city. Jesus entered the capital of Judea, Jerusalem. They lived in Rome, the capital of the Empire. Like him, they were faced with authorities of the city or the Empire.
- Like Jesus they were persecuted. The memory of Nero's terrible persecutions was very fresh in their minds and hearts.
- Like Jesus they were sometimes forced to hide. Every evening Jesus left the city where he was protected by the crowds, to go to his friend's house in a neighboring village, Bethany. Christians in Rome were forced to live and practice their religion in semi-secret.

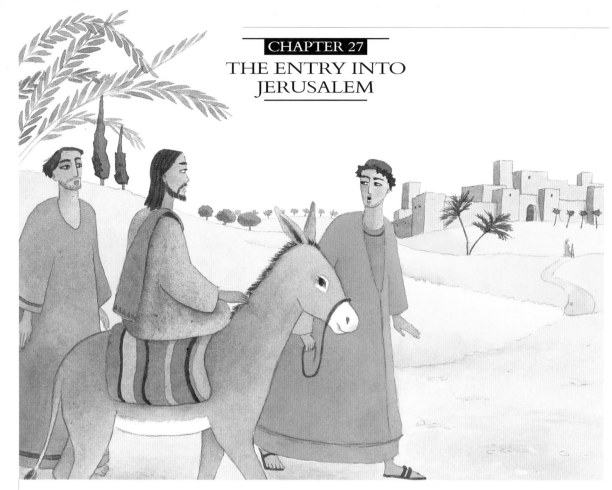

CHAPTER 27

THE ENTRY INTO JERUSALEM

THE GOSPEL

¹ Jesus and his disciples reached Bethphage and Bethany near the Mount of Olives. When they were getting close to Jerusalem, Jesus sent two of them on ahead. ² He told them, "Go into the next village. As soon as you enter it, you will find a young donkey that has never been ridden. Untie the donkey and bring it here. ³ If anyone asks why you are doing that, say, 'The Lord needs it and will soon bring it back.'"

⁴ The disciples left and found the donkey tied near a door that faced the street. While they were untying it, ⁵ some of the people standing there asked, "Why are you untying the donkey?" ⁶ They told them what Jesus had said, and the people let them take it.

⁷ The disciples led the donkey to Jesus. They put some of their clothes on its back, and Jesus got on. ⁸ Many people spread clothes on the road, while others went to cut branches from the fields.

⁹ In front of Jesus and behind him, people went along shouting,

"Hooray!
God bless the one who comes
   in the name of the Lord!
¹⁰ God bless the coming kingdom
   of our ancestor David.
Hooray for God
   in heaven above!"

¹¹ After Jesus had gone to Jerusalem, he went into the temple and looked around at everything. But since it was already late in the day, he went back to Bethany with the twelve disciples.

Mark 11.1-11

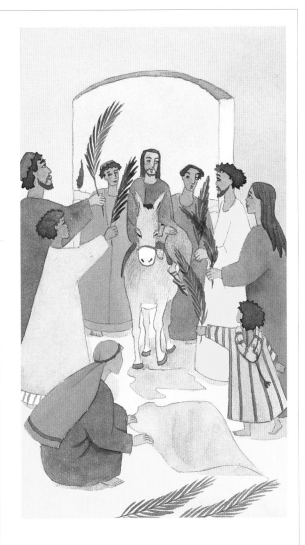

UNDERSTANDING THE TEXT

1. Look for the itinerary that Jesus followed. First list the names of the places that are mentioned in the passage and then look for them on the map of Jerusalem, page 282.

2. Look up the meaning of the following words in the glossary: *Hooray (Hosanna), donkey, David, Temple* and *Jerusalem.*

LIVING TODAY

A DIFFERENT LORD

People who thought that Jesus was a controlling master, who imposed his will on others, were mistaken. Jesus didn't come to judge the good and the wicked, to establish a strict, punitive law and to reject sinners, to weigh good and evil, or to cast down those who didn't follow him. Jesus came not to crush humans but to raise them up. He came not to throw sinners into the fire but to give them each a chance. He came not to be a terrifying master but a close friend. He came without fireworks, without a crown and without jewels. He came as a humble person who had only love to offer. He came not to rule like a king but to love like a brother. Truly, Jesus is a different Lord!

PRAISING

It is easy to praise God with words and music! But true praise is when we praise God with our whole lives. How? By trusting God even in hard times. By seeking in God the Word that gives life. By living the Gospel. By recognizing Jesus as the Lord who saves. By proclaiming, as Jesus did, that God wants everyone to be happy. If each Christian praised Jesus with words and actions, what beautiful music would be heard around the world!

INVITING JESUS IN

If we let Jesus into our hearts we have to expect changes. If we open the door to Jesus, if we invite him in, our lives begin to change. Accepting Jesus implies forgiveness of sins, welcoming the scorned, sharing with the poor, praying to our God who is in heaven, and serving our brothers and sisters with humility. We receive God's Spirit, who chases out everything that has withered away within us. If you want your life to be transformed, made new, then let the Lord Jesus in.

HUMBLY

When we welcome Jesus into our lives, his love changes our behavior. We try not to be nasty. We try not to be mean at school, at home, at work, with friends or even with strangers we meet. We try not to insist that others do exactly what we ask. Instead we try to behave humbly because we believe that others are as important as we are!

COME

Come, Lord, into our homes!
Come, there is room for you.
Come, open the door.

Come into our homes
so everyone can see
the face of God.
Come so death
doesn't have the final word.
Come stay with us
who have lost hope
and are afraid of the dark.

Come so the poor
can take their rightful place.
Come so your Word
may sing God's infinite tenderness
in our hearts.
Come to awaken in us
the desire to share
with those who are hungry.
Come so the weak
can stand with dignity
and hate is dismissed.

Come! Enter!
Our life is open to you
as a house is open
to the sun in springtime.
Come, enter.
You are our Lord!

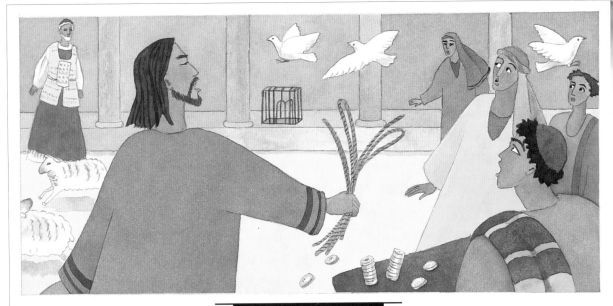

MERCHANTS CHASED FROM THE TEMPLE

IN JESUS' DAY

The Temple was in the northern part of Jerusalem, and it dominated the whole city. It didn't resemble today's churches. First of all, there was a huge square courtyard surrounded by pillars. In the center stood the sanctuary. For Jews in Jesus' day, this was the "house of God."

But this sacred place had become a loud, noisy, sometimes dishonest marketplace. Merchants selling animals set up their booths there. To pilgrims they sold animals to be sacrificed: cows, lambs, goats and doves. Nearby, moneychangers set up booths where people could exchange money. Often people arrived from different countries without the necessary Jewish currency to buy things and to pay the Temple tax.

The chief priests knew about this situation and turned a blind eye. They also profited from the situation. The large square in front of the Temple also had become a shortcut leading from one side of town to the other. Just about anything and anyone passed through there. Some pious Jews remembered the words of the prophet Jeremiah, "You are thieves, and you have made my temple your hide out" (Jeremiah 7.11), or of

Zechariah, "... there will no longer be a need to sell special pots and bowls [at the temple]" (Zechariah 14.21). When Jesus saw all of this, he got angry. He made a whip. He forced the merchants to leave. He overturned some of their tables. He chased away the animals. The chief priests were very upset. Jesus had gone too far. It was time to get rid of Jesus, who was nothing but a troublemaker.

WHEN THE GOSPELS WERE WRITTEN

Mark wrote about Jesus' behavior in the Temple to people who were living in Rome, far from Jerusalem. Some of these people had converted to Christianity from Judaism, and others from paganism.

But all of them knew that it was illegal for a non-Jew to go into the Temple. A barrier kept the Jews and the non-Jews apart; it was crossed under penalty of death.

Mark wanted to show his readers that Jesus, as he cleared the Temple of these merchants, also destroyed this barrier. This is why he reminded them of a text from the prophet Isaiah, "... my house will be known as a house of worship for all nations" (Isaiah

56.7). "All nations" doesn't mean Jews alone but includes Greeks, Romans, Africans, Gauls, etc.

Therefore Mark was saying to his readers, "See, Jesus came to open the Temple to foreigners. Like Jesus, we welcome people from all different parts of the world into our communities."

THE GOSPEL

¹⁵ After Jesus and his disciples reached Jerusalem, he went into the temple and began chasing out everyone who was selling and buying. He turned over the tables of the moneychangers and the benches of those who were selling doves. ¹⁶ Jesus would not let anyone carry things through the temple. ¹⁷ Then he taught the people and said, "The Scriptures say, 'My house should be called a place of worship for all nations.' But you have made it a place where robbers hide!"

¹⁸ The chief priests and the teachers of the Law of Moses heard what Jesus said, and they started looking for a way to kill him. They were afraid of him, because the crowds were completely amazed at his teaching.

¹⁹ That evening, Jesus and the disciples went outside the city.

Mark 11.15-19

UNDERSTANDING THE TEXT

1. Make two columns:
one that describes what the temple had become, and the other that describes what it should be.

2. Try to find the words of the ancient prophets Isaiah and Jeremiah in this passage.

3. Make three columns:
- those who are for Jesus
- those who are against Jesus
- those whose opinion we don't know.

MERCHANTS CHASED FROM THE TEMPLE

LIVING TODAY

SACRIFICES

You can't bargain with God! You can't bribe God to get your way. In Jesus' day and still today, some people think that God wants expensive gifts or painful sacrifices. Maybe people think or act this way because they are afraid of God. Perhaps they think that they must have God "on their side." What kind of God do we believe in if we must bribe or buy his favor? We can offer sacrifices without really meaning what we say — empty sacrifices, lacking love! But God is full of love. All God expects is that we love God too! Love has nothing to do with business transactions! Only one thing is important for God — that we love him with all our hearts and love our neighbors as ourselves, and that we show this through our words and actions.

A HOUSE OF PRAYER

Christians get together to praise and pray to God in churches. Churches are houses where Jesus' Gospel is proclaimed officially, in public — a message that calls us to change our lives. They are places where Jesus is also present among his people. During the Lord's Supper, or Holy Communion, (also called Eucharist in some churches — from the Greek word which means "thanksgiving"), Jesus blesses his people gathered to communicate with the One who has offered his body and blood for the life of the world. It is there that Christians throughout their lives say together, "Truly, Lord, you are our hope. You give us new life!"

AN OPEN HOUSE

Jesus' friends, those who choose to live by the Gospel, make up the Christian community: the Church. This Church isn't just a building; it is a people! Everyone is invited. There is a place ready for everyone: people of every culture, strong, weak, rich and poor. Everyone is welcome. No one is rejected. There are no barriers to separate people. Christians only want to serve God and humanity, to spread God's joy to everyone and to show the world how to participate in Jesus Christ's life.

YOUR HOUSE

*Your house is welcoming, Lord.
It is built
so that every child of this earth
feels happy there,
at home.*

*Your house is peaceful, Lord.
We have to get away
from all the noise
to hear the music of your presence
in the depths of our hearts.*

*Your house is filled with light, Lord,
that make your light
shine before our eyes,
stronger than any shadow.*

*Your house is busy, Lord,
like a place of celebration.
Your people are praying
and all the songs, cries and cares
of the earth rise up to you.*

*Here we are in your house, Lord,
to taste the joy of your great love!*

CHAPTER 29

THE STORY
OF THE THREE SERVANTS

IN JESUS' DAY

Jesus often used the image of a servant in his teachings. This word could mean "slave," but it often meant a servant who was given an important responsibility by the master. A servant was someone who was trusted by his master. Some servants were faithful and hard workers; some were unfaithful and lazy.

In the Bible, leaders (judges, prophets and kings) were considered servants of God. When Jesus talked about servants, his listeners thought about their own leaders. These leaders — high priests, scribes and Pharisees — were appointed by God to help people enter the Kingdom.

But some religious leaders were bad servants. High priests were rich and under Rome's control. Some scribes didn't explain God's Word very well. Some Pharisees thought only about obeying the Law and didn't want anything to do with ordinary people.

Jesus let them know that a day was coming when they would be held accountable for their actions. On this day God, the master, would get rid of all bad servants.

WHEN THE GOSPELS WERE WRITTEN

Matthew took Jesus' parables about servants and applied them to the lives of the early Christians. Many things had changed. Jesus was no longer among them. They had understood that Jesus was God. They addressed him as "Lord." Jesus was their master, the Lord of God's servants.

High priests no longer existed. Pharisees and scribes had less influence in these early communities. The Christians felt that they had received a treasure from God to take care of and nurture. They were the ones who could show others the way to the Kingdom. They had the "keys" to the Kingdom.

The Christians were waiting for Jesus to return. But they didn't know when he would return. They had been waiting a long time. It was like the master who left for a long trip and told his servants to take care of the estate while he was gone. It was important to remain alert, not to be afraid, and to work wisely.

Among the servants some were better suited for the job than others. Some were more dynamic, others less. Some had more skills than others. They worked with the skills they'd been given. What counted was whether they used all the skills, or talent, or energy that each had been given.

The servants knew that the day would come when they would be held accountable. On this day some would rejoice with the Lord about the work that they had done. Others would be alone and sad, trapped by a sorrow of their own making.

CHAPTER 29
THE STORY
OF THE THREE SERVANTS

THE GOSPEL

[14] The kingdom is also like what happened when a man went away and put his three servants in charge of all he owned. [15] The man knew what each servant could do. So he handed five thousand coins to the first servant, two thousand to the second, and one thousand to the third. Then he left the country.

[16] As soon as the man had gone, the servant with the five thousand coins used them to earn five thousand more. [17] The servant who had two thousand coins did the same with his money and earned two thousand more. [18] But the servant with one thousand coins dug a hole and hid his master's money in the ground.

[19] Some time later the master of those servants returned. He called them in and asked what they had done with his money. [20] The servant who had been given

five thousand coins brought them in with the five thousand that he had earned. He said, "Sir, you gave me five thousand coins, and I have earned five thousand more."

²¹ "Wonderful!" his master replied. "You are a good and faithful servant. I left you in charge of only a little, but now I will put you in charge of much more. Come and share in my happiness!"

²² Next, the servant who had been given two thousand coins came in and said, "Sir, you gave me two thousand coins, and I have earned two thousand more."

²³ "Wonderful!" his master replied. "You are a good and faithful servant. I left you in charge of only a little, but now I will put you in charge of much more. Come and share in my happiness!"

²⁴ The servant who had been given one thousand coins then came in and said, "Sir, I know that you are hard to get along with. You harvest what you don't plant and gather crops where you haven't scattered seed. ²⁵ I was frightened and went out and hid your money in the ground. Here is every single coin!"

²⁶ The master of the servant told him, "You are lazy and good-for-nothing! You know that I harvest what I don't plant and gather crops where I haven't scattered seed. ²⁷ You could have at least put my money in the bank, so that I could have earned interest on it."

²⁸ Then the master said, "Now your money will be taken away and given to the servant with ten thousand coins!"

Matthew 25.14-28

UNDERSTANDING
THE TEXT

1. Look for the word *master* and *Sir*. What do they mean when used in the parable?

2. One thousand coins represent a lot of money: over a thousand dollars. What would two or five thousand coins be worth today?

THE STORY
OF THE THREE SERVANTS

ABILITIES

We all have a treasure inside us — that's who we are! We use this treasure to do the things that we alone have the ability to do. We can think, reflect, let our minds meditate on questions and imagine solutions. We can be carried away by the beauty of a rainbow, the sound of music, or the immensity of the universe. We are all able to laugh and to improve our lives and the lives of others. We are able to choose good or evil as well as the road we would like to follow. We can create new and beautiful things. We are able to love — to reach out and forgive, to find happiness in loving and being loved, to spread joy. We each have a marvelous store of abilities. This treasure comes from God who made us all in his image.

DEVELOPING

What good is that treasure if it doesn't motivate us? What good are those riches if we don't use them? What a waste! We don't tell God, "This treasure doesn't interest me, I want something else!" God trusts us and gives us this marvelous treasure. In response to God's trust we must choose to develop our skills, to improve our abilities and see the result of our actions. What a responsibility — to use our abilities to develop the gifts that God gave us! Our other choice is to bury them and not use them at all.

SERVING

With these talents we can make something out of our lives and accomplish great things for ourselves and others. God gives us a mission — to develop our abilities and use them to serve others. This is the "service" that God asks of us. God's faithful servants use their abilities to create, with God, a world where everyone feels loved, a world in God's image!

BASKET

*My basket is overflowing
— with love to share,
with joy to increase,
with a vivid imagination,
with dreams to realize,
with words that sing,
with smiles to share,
with poems to write,
with brand new ideas!*

*Thank you, Lord,
for all that you have given me.*

*Look, Lord!
My basket is overflowing.
I grasp it, full of life,
and without hesitation
I give wholeheartedly
of what you have entrusted to me.*

*Look, Lord!
From this basket
I offer everything
that you placed here
and also everything
that I have added.
Everything will be shared
generously to bring joy
to our world.*

CHAPTER 30

THE LAST JUDGMENT

IN JESUS' DAY

Life isn't always rosy. In Jesus' day some people were able to save money, to enjoy life and to live in luxury. On the other hand, some asked each morning, "What am I going to eat today? How will I warm myself tonight?" Many peasants were burdened by debts and taxes. Many sick people were unable to get help. Poor and sick people remained trapped in their isolation. Foreigners traveling through a strange country were at risk. And what happened to the widows and orphans? Faced with these miserable conditions, people did one of three things:

- They said that the Romans were responsible. This was partly true. The answer was to plan a rebellion against Rome. They always failed; Rome was too strong.

- They did nothing. They would wait for God to intervene to reestablish justice. Many hoped that this day would come soon and that the good would be rewarded and the evil punished.

- They tried to relieve the misery where they could. In Jesus' day this was called "doing good works," such as feeding the hungry, clothing the naked, welcoming foreigners, visiting the sick, burying the dead, educating orphans.

What did Jesus do?

- He refused to become involved in a rebellion against Rome. That wasn't his mission.

- He spoke of the Son of Man. This was a mysterious person — according to what the prophet Daniel had said — whom many people were expecting. He would come in glory, riding on the clouds. He would judge all living beings and reestablish justice.

- He gave real help to those who were in need. He became the servant of the weak, the sick, foreigners, children, widows and the hungry.

WHEN THE GOSPELS WERE WRITTEN

Matthew is the only author of the gospels to paint a picture of the last judgment. This description is found in the final speech Jesus gave before his crucifixion. Matthew — who wrote his gospel around 80 A.D. — tried to answer some of his readers' questions:

- Many of his readers were of Jewish origin. They were waiting for a judgement in favor of the poor and the lowly. Matthew showed them that "all nations" would be judged. There were no more distinctions.

- Some people were happy just to pray. They cried, "Lord, Lord!" but they didn't do anything to help others. Matthew said to them, "Practice good works, as in Judaism." But he included another work in the list — visiting prisoners. This was more dangerous, but it was important to give everything.

- Others were dreamers and looked to the future. They were waiting for Jesus to return. Everyone knew that this Son of Man, who would come to judge humanity, was Jesus himself. Matthew said to them, "Stop dreaming! Your brother and sister need your help today!"

- Some asked, "Where is Jesus found?" Matthew reminded them of this sentence that Jesus said: "What you do to the least among us, you do to me!" You can find Jesus today when you serve your brothers and sisters.

THE GOSPEL

31 When the Son of Man comes in his glory with all of his angels, he will sit on his royal throne. 32 The people of all nations will be brought before him, and he will separate them, as shepherds separate their sheep from their goats.

33 He will place the sheep on his right and the goats on his left. 34 Then the king will say to those on his right, "My father has blessed you! Come and receive the kingdom that was prepared for you before the world was created. 35 When I was hungry, you gave me something to eat, and when I was thirsty, you gave me something to drink. When I was a stranger, you welcomed me, 36 and when I was naked, you gave me clothes to wear. When I was sick, you took care of me, and when I was in jail, you visited me."

37 Then the ones who pleased the Lord will ask, "When did we give you something to eat or drink? 38 When did we welcome you as a stranger or give you clothes to wear 39 or visit you while you were sick or in jail?"

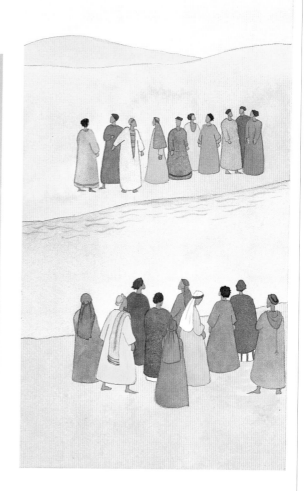

⁴⁰ The king will answer, "Whenever you did it for any of my people, no matter how unimportant they seemed, you did it for me."

⁴¹ Then the king will say to those on his left, "Get away from me! You are under God's curse. Go into the everlasting fire prepared for the devil and his angels! ⁴² I was hungry, but you did not give me anything to eat, and I was thirsty, but you did not give me anything to drink. ⁴³ I was a stranger, but you did not welcome me, and I was naked, but you did not give me any clothes to wear. I was sick and in jail, but you did not take care of me."

⁴⁴ Then the people will ask, "Lord, when did we fail to help you when you were hungry or thirsty or a stranger or naked or sick or in jail?" ⁴⁵ The king will say to them, "Whenever you failed to help any of my people, no matter how unimportant they seemed, you failed to do it for me."

⁴⁶ Then Jesus said, "Those people will be punished forever. But the ones who pleased God will have eternal life."

Matthew 25.31-46

UNDERSTANDING THE TEXT

1. Look for all the words that describe misery.

2. Look for all the titles that are given to the "Son of Man."

3. What sentence seems the most important to you, the key sentence in the passage?

4. Look up the meanings of the following words in the glossary: *Son of Man, glory, angel, devil.*

THE MANY FACES OF CHRIST

Where do we see Jesus' face? On the faces of the living! We need to look for Jesus' face in the people around us! We need to find signs of his presence in their lives. But most of all in the faces of those whose lives are painful or unhappy, who don't have their share of happiness. People who are hungry, who do not receive fair wages, who are suffering and alone in our inner cities and countryside. People who live in shanty towns, who are forced to beg, who do not cry out in protest in order to safeguard what little they possess. People who suffer constantly, who live on the street, who look for food in the garbage, who are in prison and have no one to talk to. People who are persecuted because of their culture or religion, or ignored because they are elderly. People we ridicule because their bodies are deformed, who never have any luck. These people who seem "unimportant" want to live like human beings. They are everywhere, crying for help. These are the faces of Christ!

SEEING

We find Christ in prayer, in worship celebrations in reflection and when we reflect on the Gospel! But to see Jesus, all we have to do is open our eyes and hearts to the faces we see everyday on the street. We find Jesus in our daily lives. Seeing Christ in the "unimportant" faces scarred by life should make us ask questions: "But how can an entire country have nothing while others waste so much? Why are strangers rejected? Why are some people treated as though they were evil? How can it be?"

SERVING CHRIST

Is there any other way to serve Christ than by serving other human beings? Is there any other way to love Christ than by loving one another, fighting against anything that degrades people, and working to lessen the suffering in the world? We can't accept anything that denies respect to women and men. We must work with others who try to change the world. We show our faithfulness to Christ by working for justice and for an equal sharing of happiness.

OPEN

Open my eyes, Lord,
so I can see you
in your dirty clothes,
on the sidewalk,
holding out your hand.
So I can see you
crying in despair
because you were treated
as a "dirty immigrant."
So I can see you
in your country
suffering from famine,
begging for help to plant, to build.

Open my lips, Lord,
so that I can cry out,
"That's enough! Come, friends,
we have to pick up our Christ,
and set our brothers and sisters
on their feet!"

Open my hands, Lord,
so I may work
to make a world
where each human being
has enough food
and enough respect.
Where every human being
can shout, "It is wonderful
to be alive in this world!"

THE LAST SUPPER

IN JESUS' DAY

Passover was an important Jewish holiday. At Passover the people remembered the time when Moses and the Israelite people were freed from slavery in Egypt. Many pilgrims flocked to Jerusalem.

For an entire week everyone ate bread without yeast. This tradition reminded the people of their ancestors' quick departure from Egypt. They hadn't had time to wait for the dough to rise. Another tradition was killing of the paschal lamb. The lamb was eaten during a commemorative meal. The blood of this lamb was a reminder of God's covenant with the people of Israel.

Jesus arrived in Jerusalem to celebrate Passover with his disciples. He had been wanting to share the paschal meal with them for a long time. A friend offered them his house. The disciples prepared the lamb, the unleavened bread, bitter herbs and wine. They were together on the evening of the 14th of Nisan (April). Judas, the traitor, was also present.

At the end of the meal Jesus broke and shared the bread and invited the disciples to drink from the cup. What Jesus said surprised them — by this bread and wine he would always be present with his friends! The meal ended with the singing of a psalm. Then they left the house and went down to a garden at the foot of the Mount of Olives. This was their last meal with Jesus; they would never forget it.

WHEN THE GOSPELS WERE WRITTEN

After Jesus' death and resurrection, the disciples and the early Christians often got together. They remembered the last meal they had shared with Jesus. They took bread and wine; they repeated the actions and words of the Master. They gave thanks to God, as Jesus had. Later these meetings would be called the "Lord's Supper" or "Holy Communion" — in some churches they are also called "Eucharist," a Greek word which means "thanksgiving," because Jesus "gave thanks" when he was sharing this meal with his disciples.

They also knew that this last meal with Jesus had preceded his arrest and execution on a cross by only a few hours. They remembered what Jesus had told the disciples about the wine he shared with them: "This is my blood, and with it God makes his agreement with you." This agreement — we also say "Covenant" — meant that Christians would no longer sacrifice animals for Passover. Instead, they would renew this covenant at a meal of bread and wine.

When Matthew wrote about the last supper with Jesus he showed the early Christians that during their gatherings they were telling in a very special way about his death until he would come again (1 Corinthians 11.26).

CHAPTER 31
THE LAST SUPPER

THE GOSPEL

[17] On the first day of the Festival of Thin Bread, Jesus' disciples came to him and asked, "Where do you want us to prepare the Passover meal?"

[18] Jesus told them to go to a certain man in the city and tell him, "Our teacher says, 'My time has come! I want to eat the Passover meal with my disciples in your home.'" [19] They did as Jesus told them and prepared the meal.

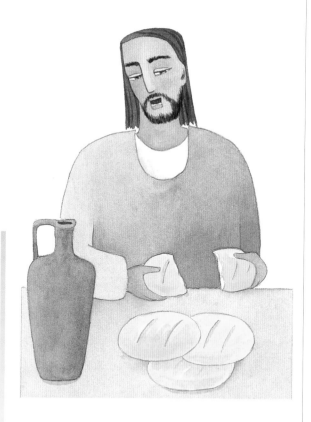

20-21 When Jesus was eating with his twelve disciples that evening, he said, "One of you will surely hand me over to my enemies."

22 The disciples were very sad, and each one said to Jesus, "Lord, you can't mean me!"

23 He answered, "One of you... who has eaten with me from this dish will betray me..."

26 During the meal Jesus took some bread in his hands. He blessed the bread and broke it. Then he gave it to his disciples and said, "Take this and eat it. This is my body."

27 Jesus picked up a cup of wine and gave thanks to God. He then gave it to his disciples and said, "Take this and drink it. 28 This is my blood, and with it God makes his agreement with you. It will be poured out, so that many people will have their sins forgiven. 29 From now on I am not going to drink any wine, until I drink new wine with you in my Father's kingdom." 30 Then they sang a hymn and went out to the Mount of Olives.

Matthew 26.17-23, 26-30

UNDERSTANDING THE TEXT

1. Look through this passage for words that you hear in church during the "Lord's Supper."

2. Look on the map of Jerusalem for the house where the meal was held and for the olive garden.

3. Look up the meanings of the following words in the glossary: *agreement (covenant), Festival of Thin Bread, Twelve, psalm (hymn)* and *kingdom.*

4. Reread the chapter in this book that talks about the "multiplication of the bread," pages 111 to 115.

LIVING
TODAY

Breaking

When we break bread we divide it into pieces. It doesn't remain whole. It is broken so that a lot of people can share it. In order to share we must break the bread into pieces. People who eat this broken bread are united or joined together by the life force of this bread that they shared. When we receive this bread, we in turn want to share some with those who don't have any. Breaking bread can also remind us of a wound — we tear the bread in half! But isn't that necessary so many can share the same loaf?

Jesus chose to be broken like the bread. To be torn apart in order to reveal and share his great love. To be shared in order to offer his life for everyone. We, too, can break our lives, tear them apart and share them with others; we do this out of love to increase the happiness of others.

Pouring

When people pour wine, it's as if they're pouring out celebration and joy. The wine contains the light of the sun and the taste of the earth. Because of the abuse of wine and alcohol, wine no longer has this meaning in many places and churches today, but those who share it in moderation want others to celebrate with them.

Jesus chose to be like wine that is poured out so he could share God's joy with the world. He shared his works, his actions, his entire life and his death to invite everybody to God's celebration. Is it possible to pour out your life like a joyous wine without first being crushed and squeezed like the grapes?

"The Lord's Supper"

Christians remember in a very special way the Lord's Supper. His death and resurrection are their hope today — Jesus Christ is the light of their lives. Today, celebrating the Lord's Supper means to walk along the difficult path with him and to accept being broken and poured out for the joy of the world. Sharing this meaningful meal with others is to declare, "I want to be like Christ, who gave his life for me, and to do for others what he did for me."

THANK YOU

For the bread
that gives everlasting life
and nourishment so we can love
God with all our strength
and our neighbor as ourselves.
For offering us your body,
thank you, our Lord!

For the wine
that gives everlasting joy
and strength to spread happiness
among all our brothers and sisters.
For offering us your blood,
thank you, our Lord!

For the Lord's Supper
that proclaims your glory.
For you, Christ Jesus,
who came to invite all the children
of the world to your celebration.
For you, Christ Jesus,
who are always with us,
thank you!

CHAPTER 32

GETHSEMANE

IN JESUS' DAY

Judas, one of the twelve apostles, was not happy. Maybe he had hoped Jesus would lead a rebellion against Rome and establish a new kingdom. Judas wanted to see results. He also liked money, and sometimes he stole. So one day Judas made a bargain with the chief priests who were upset by Jesus. Judas was paid thirty pieces of silver for leading them to Jesus. (Thirty pieces of silver was the price for a slave. It was as much as the salary for thirty days' work.)

During the last supper Judas found out where they would be going next. He left quietly to tell the chief priests and the troops where they could take Jesus prisoner. Because it was dark and they wouldn't recognize Jesus, they agreed on a sign. Judas was to greet Jesus with a kiss, a common form of greeting.

After the meal the eleven apostles and Jesus went to a garden with olive trees and an olive press, at the foot of a hill. The garden was called Gethsemane. Jesus was aware of who and what were conspiring against him. He knew that his final hour was near. When he needed the support of his friends, Peter, James and John, Jesus found they had fallen fast asleep.

Jesus was sad and filled with deep anxiety. So he prayed to God — he asked whether what lay ahead could be avoided. But he accepted it willingly. Jesus was alone; his disciples were sleeping. The traitor arrived. The kiss of friendship became a kiss of betrayal. Jesus was taken prisoner until his death, the next day.

WHEN THE GOSPELS WERE WRITTEN

When Mark (around 65 A.D.) wrote the story of Jesus' arrest, many things had changed. Judas had killed himself out of despair (around 30 A.D.). Matthias had taken Judas' place in the group of twelve. Peter had probably been executed as a Christian under the Emperor Nero (around 64 A.D.). James had been martyred by the sword under Herod (in 44 A.D.). John was responsible for the Christians in Ephesus (Turkey today). The Christians in Jerusalem hadn't forgotten the Garden of Gethsemane where Jesus had experienced such anguish.

As they read the gospel, Christians could understand that even the most faithful disciples had moments of weakness. Peter, James and John had been with Jesus on the mountain during the Transfiguration. They hadn't really understood what Jesus wanted. Now they were sound asleep in the Garden of Gethsemane. These were nonetheless disciples who later gave their lives for Christ. Mark wanted to show that though things didn't start off well, after the resurrection anything was possible.

Mark wrote that Jesus used an odd word when speaking with God. This is the only time in the gospel that the word "Abba," meaning "Father" or "Daddy," is used. Jesus spoke to God as a child speaks to his father. Christians should understand by this that Jesus is the Son of God. They, too, are invited to pray with this word, "… we become his children and call him our Father" (Romans 8.15).

GETHSEMANE

THE GOSPEL

32 Jesus went with his disciples to a place called Gethsemane, and he told them, "Sit here while I pray."

33 Jesus took along Peter, James, and John. He was sad and troubled and 34 told them, "I am so sad that I feel as if I am dying. Stay here and keep awake with me."

35-36 Jesus walked on a little way. Then he knelt down on the ground and prayed, "Father, if it is possible, don't let this happen to me! Father, you can do anything. Don't make me suffer by having me drink from this cup. But do what you want, and not what I want."

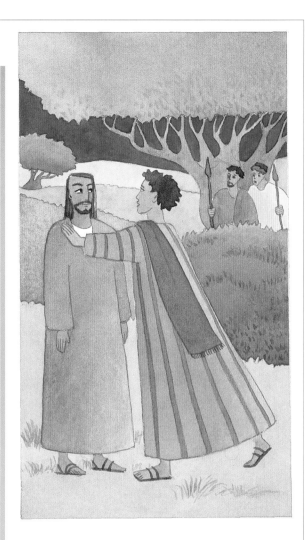

³⁷ When Jesus came back and found the disciples sleeping, he said to Simon Peter, "Are you asleep? Can't you stay awake for just one hour? ³⁸ Stay awake and pray that you won't be tested. You want to do what is right, but you are weak."

³⁹ Jesus went back and prayed the same prayer. ⁴⁰ But when he returned to the disciples, he found them sleeping again. They simply could not keep their eyes open, and they did not know what to say.

⁴¹ When Jesus returned to the disciples the third time, he said, "Are you still sleeping and resting? Enough of that! The time has come for the Son of Man to be handed over to sinners. ⁴² Get up! Let's go. The one who will betray me is already here."

⁴³ Jesus was still speaking, when Judas the betrayer came up. He was one of the twelve disciples, and a mob of men armed with swords and clubs were with him. They had been sent by the chief priests, the nation's leaders, and the teachers of the Law of Moses. ⁴⁴ Judas had told them ahead of time, "Arrest the man I greet with a kiss. Tie him up tight and lead him away."

⁴⁵ Judas walked right up to Jesus and said, "Teacher!" Then Judas kissed him, ⁴⁶ and the men grabbed Jesus and arrested him.

Mark 14.32-46

UNDERSTANDING THE TEXT

1. Look for the names of the different groups of people who are angry with Jesus.

2. Look for all the words that are similar to "fear" or "anxiety."

3. Reread the sentences that Jesus speaks. Pick the one that means the most to you.

4. Look at the attitudes that Peter, James and John have in the passage of the Transfiguration, pages 122 to 123.

LIVING TODAY

ALONE

We think we have friends we can count on or a family that will support us. But sometimes our friends or family aren't there when we really need them; they don't have the time, they're too busy with something else or they say that it's better to just get along on our own. We find ourselves alone, abandoned in the night. Alone and confronted by people who would like to destroy our reputation — no one to speak for us. Alone in the hospital bed — no one to visit us. Alone in our old age — no one to offer us comfort. Alone in grief and sadness — no one to console us. Alone and faced with difficult situations — no one to walk with us. Alone and discouraged — no one to pick us up. Alone with injustice — no one to defend us. Abandoned. How can I struggle alone when my friends have fallen asleep and have left me to carry very heavy burdens? Death surrounds me with a net of darkness and shadows. Jesus experienced solitude. As we do. Jesus will never leave us alone.

FEAR

Fear can paralyze our minds, bodies and hearts. Fear can remove any hope we have. Our lives can be darkened by fear. Fear can take away our desire to fight and seem to paralyze our spirits. Our hearts pound with fear; joy is driven out. We feel worse when we are alone because fear holds us captive.

We feel dread when faced with an incurable illness; anguish when we are faced with death; confusion when we fail; fear when we are faced with people who judge us; horror for those who are locked up and tortured for their ideas; despair when we lack food; worry when we think we may never find work; the terror of a beaten child; concern for the innocent people to whom no one listens — we face these fears and others in our lives!
Jesus experienced these fears. As we do. Jesus will never abandon us to fear.

TRUST

God's love for us and our love for God empower us in spite of the loneliness and fear we experience. Trust grows through the shared love. Trust shines through even in the dark of night. We cling to God as we once clung to our parents' arms. When everything seems to be against us, God is looking out for us. No evil can defeat God's children. Jesus had trust. And even when Jesus had to confront death alone — as if he were abandoned by God — God didn't abandon him, and he will never abandon us.

YOU!

When happiness,
that shines like the sun,
disappears from our sky
in times of trouble,
when we are abandoned
or betrayed,
betrayed or when we sin,
you remain close to us,
Lord of great faithfulness!

When suffering grips us
like never before,
when our lives are taken over
by unhappiness
and there is no one
there to comfort us,
you remain close to us,
Lord of mighty help!

Lord,
we need your love
that supports
and gives us new life.
You are with us
in times of darkness and fear.
Be with us, Lord of great trust!

BEFORE PILATE

IN JESUS' DAY

Pilate was the Roman governor of Judea from 25 to 36 A.D. He was responsible for seeing that things went smoothly during the Passover celebration. Above all, Pilate wanted to avoid a revolution. During Jesus' time there were many Jews who wanted to be freed from the Roman occupation and put their own king back in power.

Jesus spent a terrible night in prison after being betrayed by Judas and arrested by the soldiers. He was dragged from judge to judge. Very early that morning the High Council, which did not have the right to execute anyone, turned Jesus over to Pilate. Pilate found this very awkward. He didn't want to cause an uprising. He was afraid of what Rome might think. He didn't understand the Jewish people's desire to be free. But he understood that there was no evil in Jesus.

It was a Passover tradition that the governor could free one prisoner at the people's request. The crowd approached Pilate's palace to ask for freedom for one prisoner. Pilate thought that he had found the solution to his problem. He asked the crowd to choose between two prisoners: Barrabas or Jesus. Barrabas had been involved in a plot against Rome; two people had died. Jesus, on the other hand, hadn't done anything wrong. Despite the accusations of the chief priests (that Jesus claimed to be the king of the Jews), Jesus wasn't dangerous to Rome. Pilate was sure that the crowd would choose Jesus.

But he had forgotten about the influence of the chief priests. They turned the crowd against Jesus. The crowd cried that Barrabas be freed and that Jesus die. Pilate, weak and indecisive, turned Jesus over to the executioners to be beaten and nailed on a cross. In those days prisoners were tied to poles and beaten with whips made from strips of leather with little pieces of lead or bone attached to the leather.

WHEN THE GOSPELS WERE WRITTEN

Mark was in Rome when he wrote about Jesus' trial. At this time in Palestine, about 1800 miles from Rome, the Jewish people were rising up against the Roman occupation. The war lasted four years and thousands died. It led to the destruction of Jerusalem and the Temple. The revolutionaries did not succeed in putting their own king back in power.

When Mark wrote his gospel, the Christians in Rome had just lived though terrible persecutions. They knew how it felt to be judged and condemned for crimes that they had not committed! They could feel very close to Jesus, who was dragged from court to court and condemned for no valid reason.

The Christians in Rome were trying to live in peace with the Roman authorities. They didn't rebel as did the Jews in Jerusalem. This explains why Mark showed that the Roman governor, Pilate, was not the person responsible for Jesus' death. In fact, Pilate had even tried to save Jesus. For Mark, the people who were responsible were the chief priests who had manipulated the crowds. Reading this, the Roman authorities were less suspicious of the Christians living in Rome.

BEFORE PILATE

THE GOSPEL

¹ Early the next morning the chief priests, the nation's leaders, and the teachers of the Law of Moses met together with the whole Jewish council. They tied up Jesus and led him off to Pilate.

² He asked Jesus, "Are you the king of the Jews?"

"Those are your words," Jesus answered.

³ The chief priests brought many charges against Jesus. ⁴ Then Pilate questioned him again, "Don't you have anything to say? Don't you hear what crimes they say you have done?" ⁵ But Jesus did not answer, and Pilate was amazed.

⁶ During Passover, Pilate always freed one prisoner chosen by the people. ⁷ And at that time there was a prisoner named Barabbas. He and some others had been arrested for murder during a riot. ⁸ The crowd now came and asked Pilate to set a prisoner free, just as he usually did.

⁹ Pilate asked them, "Do you want me to free the king of the Jews?" ¹⁰ Pilate knew that the chief priests had brought Jesus to him because they were jealous.

¹¹ But the chief priests told the crowd to ask Pilate to free Barabbas.

¹² Then Pilate asked the crowd, "What do you want me to do with this man you say is the king of the Jews?"

¹³ They yelled, "Nail him to a cross!"

¹⁴ Pilate asked, "But what crime has he done?"

"Nail him to a cross!" they yelled even louder.

¹⁵ Pilate wanted to please the crowd. So he set Barabbas free. Then he ordered his soldiers to beat Jesus with a whip and nail him to a cross.

Mark 15.1-15

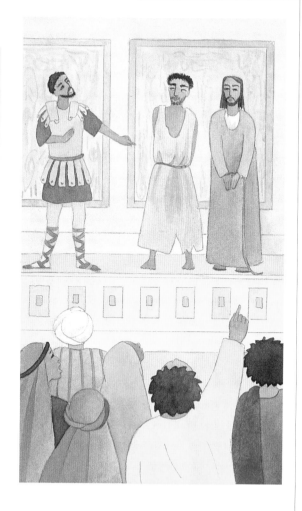

UNDERSTANDING THE TEXT

1. Look in the passage for who was "tied up," who was "led off" and who was "set free."

2. In this passage, who calls Jesus the "king of the Jews?"

3. Which adjectives would you use to describe Pilate: courageous, cowardly, weak, political, sly or intelligent?

4. On the map of Jerusalem look for the place where Pilate might have lived (page 228).

LIVING
TODAY

COWARDLY

Everyone acts like a coward at some time or another. We act like cowards when we think it's the only way to protect ourselves and to protect our advantage. It's too bad if others get hurt, but… Instead of standing up for people who are being ridiculed, we choose to turn away — we might be made fun of, too. We choose to ignore people who have broken the law; we reject people with a bad name. We don't want to be seen with someone who has just been released from prison. We don't stand up for our opinions in public, or we don't admit that we're Christians. We pretend we don't see that evil things are happening. Sometimes entire governments are cowardly — to keep voters, they allow persecution and intolerance to shape their countries. Being cowardly means not speaking out and not challenging injustice, out of selfishness. Jesus was a victim of human, cowardly behavior!

MANIPULATING THE CROWD

Dictators and politicians know that they can do what they want with a crowd! When people are together in a crowd, it's hard to speak out and to be different. It's much easier to go along with the others. A crowd can be manipulated — to hate foreigners, to demand death for an innocent victim. A crowd can be manipulated — to act from a false sense of superiority or from a racist view. We are manipulated to buy certain products, to believe certain ideas, to look out for ourselves and not others, to find happiness in physical beauty or other externals. A crowd can be manipulated with surveys, ads, styles, television, newspapers or persuasive speeches. Jesus was a victim of a crowd who was manipulated, too.

TORTURE

Throughout the world, people are condemned by mock courts because their thoughts and words are considered dangerous by the leaders of the countries. People call for equality, for land for the poor, and for equal rights. People are put into prison because they want to practice their religion or because they challenge injustice, theft and corruption among their leaders. They are tortured by those in power who hope to silence their calls for freedom. Can we live with this happening around us? Being Christian means fighting with others to challenge and to stop these practices. Jesus was a victim of torture, too!

HERE THEY ARE

*Here you are, Lord, persecuted
because you have no country
to call your own and no passport.
Because you are black, white, yellow
or red; Christian or Jew.
For no reason at all!*

*Here you are, Lord, before the court
with your head hanging low.
Facing those who condemned you:
"That will teach him to think
differently from the way we do!"*

*Here you are, Lord, in the square,
with your hands tied,
a pawn handed over
to the executioners, "That will teach
him to speak out against us!"*

*We can't just leave you like this!
With our words, shouts and actions,
with our prayers and petitions,
we will free you!*

*And here you are, Lord,
no longer prisoner,
coming out of the court,
coming out of the cave!
You are not alone!
Many others are walking with you
into the sunlight.
You lay your wounded hands
on them and say, "Here they are!
Look at them!
These are my brothers and sisters!"*

THE CRUCIFIXION

IN JESUS' DAY

According to Roman law a condemned person had to carry the instrument that would be used to put him to death. Jesus had to carry the wooden beam that would be part of his cross. Weakened by the beatings and wearing a crown of thorns on his head, Jesus was barely able to walk the one-third of a mile that separated the court and the place of execution. The place where executions took place was located outside the city gates. It was a small rocky hill that looked like a bald skull. This is where it got its name, "Golgotha" (which means "skull" in Aramaic).

Crucifixion was a terrible punishment. Nails were driven through the wrists of the condemned person to hold him to the horizontal beam of the cross. Then this beam was lifted up and attached to a vertical beam that was already fixed in the ground. His feet were nailed to this vertical beam. All the weight of his body rested on these wounds. No vital organ was touched. The suffering and agony could last a very long time. A sedative, a drink of wine and myrrh, was offered to the condemned. Jesus refused it. Normally those who were crucified died from suffocation as the body's weight compressed the lung cavity.

Crucifixion was a humiliating punishment, reserved for slaves, traitors and revolutionaries. Those who were crucified were on display, naked, suffering and dying, for everyone who went by to see. It was shameful for them, for their families and their friends. A sign indicating why they were being crucified was placed above their heads, at the top of the cross.

The disciples ran away. They were afraid. They ran and hid. Only one of them remained — John. He stood at the cross with Mary and the women who followed Jesus.

WHEN THE GOSPELS WERE WRITTEN

John tells us about Jesus' crucifixion. He wrote his account toward the end of the first century, a few decades after the crucifixion. Before he wrote anything, John meditated often on the events and spoke of them. In his gospel he didn't describe the details but only what he thought was most important for his readers.

John didn't describe the terrible suffering that Jesus endured on the cross. His version is calm and serene. He wanted to show that Jesus died on the cross for all of humanity. This is why he described the words on the sign that was hung at the top of the cross: "Jesus of Nazareth, King of the Jews." The words were written in Hebrew (the official Jewish language), Latin (the official Roman language) and Greek (the language of educated people and foreigners). They could all see that Jesus was a king. But not a king on a throne. A king on the cross. A king who gave his life for the people he loved.

Like the other gospel writers, John showed that it was the women who were with Jesus until the end. As he wrote, John was thinking about what was happening in his day. Christians were meeting in houses to remember the Lord. Women of faith were always there as they had been at the foot of the cross.

John is the only one to tell us that Mary, Jesus' mother, was also present on Golgotha. After Jesus died, Mary took care of John and he of her. When he wrote his gospel, John showed how Mary was a faithful witness of Jesus Christ, present at the beginning of his ministry (John 2) until his death, how she saw him risen from the dead and was there when the Church was forming.

THE CRUCIFIXION

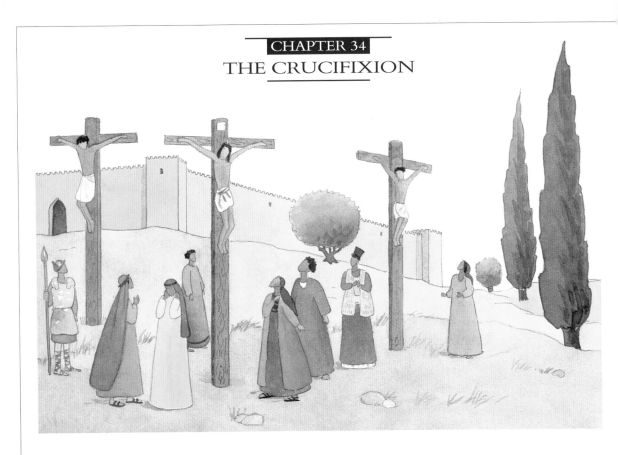

THE GOSPEL

Jesus was taken away, [17] and he carried his cross to a place known as "The Skull." In Aramaic this place is called "Golgotha." [18] There Jesus was nailed to the cross, and on each side of him a man was also nailed to a cross.

[19] Pilate ordered the charge against Jesus to be written on a board and put above the cross. It read, "Jesus of Nazareth, King of the Jews." [20] The words were written in Hebrew, Latin, and Greek.

The place where Jesus was taken wasn't far from the city, and many of the Jewish people read the charge against him. [21] So the chief priests went to Pilate and said, "Why did you write that he is King of the Jews? You should have written, 'He claimed to be King of the Jews.'"

²² But Pilate told them, "What is written will not be changed!"

²³ After the soldiers had nailed Jesus to the cross, they divided up his clothes into four parts, one for each of them. But his outer garment was made from a single piece of cloth, and it did not have any seams. ²⁴ The soldiers said to each other, "Let's not rip it apart. We will gamble to see who gets it." This happened so that the Scriptures would come true, which say,

> "They divided up my clothes
> and gambled
>   for my garments."

The soldiers then did what they had decided.

²⁵ Jesus' mother stood beside his cross with her sister and Mary the wife of Clopas. Mary Magdalene was standing there too. ²⁶ When Jesus saw his mother and his favorite disciple with her, he said to his mother, "This man is now your son." ²⁷ Then he said to the disciple, "She is now your mother." From then on, that disciple took her into his own home.

John 19.17-27

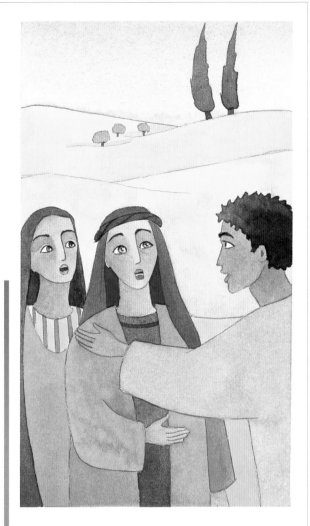

UNDERSTANDING THE TEXT

1. Look for Golgotha on the map of Jerusalem (page 228).

2. Make a list of all the people mentioned in the passage (except Jesus) and group them according to the following categories:
- those who were responsible for Jesus' death
- those who executed him
- those who were indifferent
- his faithful followers and friends.

LIVING
TODAY

THE CRUCIFIED

Today people are not crucified on a hill; no nails or crosses are used. But we see people crucified all around the world today — the countries that we abandon to famine, people who have lost their freedom and are left to beg in order to survive, refugees without land or money, people living in shelters, families torn apart by war, human beings who are beaten and executed under the pretext of establishing order, people who are poor and who have no chance of escaping their situation — without hope, without love, full of misery, sick people who can't handle it any more. They are crucified! And Christ Jesus with them!

A LORD OF LOVE

Here is our God — on the cross! God would not have accepted the cross if he had wanted to dominate or show his power. It was Jesus' desire to give people happiness that led him to this. When we see Jesus hanging on a cross, we say that God's love is certainly strange. Jesus was born in a stable; he became one of us; Jesus washed his disciples' feet; and now Jesus let himself be stripped of his clothing, broken and exposed so that everyone might find hope. On the cross we see God. Out of tenderness God is prepared to do everything for humanity. Glory doesn't interest God, or he wouldn't have accepted nails and beatings; gold doesn't interest him, or he wouldn't have tolerated being torn apart on rough wood. What interests our God is not to receive, but to give everything! To offer himself completely for the world. What a Lord of love!

THE CROSS: THE FIRST CHRISTIAN SIGN

The cross became the sign by which those who believed in the crucified Christ recognized each other. With this sign they proclaimed that God's love had entered our world. The cross was the first sign of a new world order where people fought hate with forgiveness, where people shared with others, where people turned to God as a parent, where everyone was accepted, where the hearts of men and women escaped the power of evil, and where the powers of death were overcome.

OPEN ARMS

Here you are, Jesus,
our Lord and God,
with wide-open arms
that proclaim
to all living creatures,
"See, God's love
can embrace us all."

Here you are, Christ,
our Lord and our God,
with wide-open arms
that proclaim to all living creatures,
"Come, follow me!
Nothing can get in our way.
Through the crucifixion
I will push aside evil and death
and will lead you to eternal life!"

Here we are, Jesus Christ,
kneeling before you
to look to you and say,
"Thank you,
our Lord and our God!"

CHAPTER 35

DEATH
AND THE TOMB

IN JESUS' DAY

WHEN THE GOSPELS WERE WRITTEN

Jesus was crucified about noon. As he hung on the cross, he was able to say a word from time to time when he found the strength to overcome his agony. He forgave his executioners. He comforted the two other men who had been crucified with him. He told John to look after his mother. At 3:00 p.m. Jesus cried out and gave up his spirit.

What should be done with the body? Ordinarily the bodies of condemned people were thrown in a ditch belonging to the court. Joseph of Arimathea, a member of the High Council, intervened. He had been present when Jesus was condemned. He hadn't agreed with the decision.

Joseph asked for and was given Jesus' body. He laid Jesus in a brand new tomb that had been dug in the rock wall of his garden near Golgotha. Jesus' body was laid on a stone bench inside the tomb. It was getting late. There was no time to anoint him till after the Sabbath. In the meantime the tomb was sealed with a large, round stone shaped precisely for this purpose.

The Sabbath began that night. Already the town was aglow with lights to celebrate that occasion. Jesus' friends were overcome with pain and discouragement. But they had to face the facts — the one in whom they had placed all their hope was dead.

A few decades later, when Luke tells of Jesus' death, what does he want his readers to understand?

- This death opened for all men and women, the way to God. The Temple was seen as God's dwelling place. The "Most Holly Place" was separated from the rest of the Temple by a curtain. Only the high priest could go there, and only once a year. When Luke says — in a very expressive way — that when Jesus died the curtain of the Temple was torn apart, he wants to show that there was no longer anything that separated humans beings from God. Everyone has free access to God.

- Believing in Jesus who died on a cross isn't crazy. However, when the disciples spoke of Jesus' death, many people were scandalized: "How can we follow someone who died on a cross like a slave?" Others made fun, "You have to be crazy to believe that God would let himself be crucified." When Luke told of Jesus' death, he showed that among the people who saw him die, many were changed. Curious spectators departed beating their chests as a sign of repentance. The Roman captain recognized Jesus' Godliness. And a member of the High Council had the courage to show that he didn't agree with the decision that his colleagues had made.

DEATH
AND THE TOMB

THE GOSPEL

[44] Around noon the sky turned dark and stayed that way until the middle of the afternoon. [45] The sun stopped shining, and the curtain in the temple split down the middle. [46] Jesus shouted, "Father, I put myself in your hands!" Then he died.

[47] When the Roman officer saw what had happened, he praised God and said, "Jesus must really have been a good man!"

[48] A crowd had gathered to see the terrible sight. Then after they had seen it, they felt brokenhearted and went home. [49] All of Jesus' close friends and the women who had come with him from Galilee stood at a distance and watched.

⁵⁰⁻⁵¹ There was a man named Joseph, who was from Arimathea in Judea. Joseph was a good and honest man, and he was eager for God's kingdom to come. He was also a member of the council, but he did not agree with what they had decided.

⁵² Joseph went to Pilate and asked for Jesus' body. ⁵³ He took the body down from the cross and wrapped it in fine cloth. Then he put it in a tomb that had been cut out of solid rock and had never been used. ⁵⁴ It was Friday, and the Sabbath was about to begin.

⁵⁵ The women who had come with Jesus from Galilee followed Joseph and watched how Jesus' body was placed in the tomb. ⁵⁶ Then they went to prepare some sweet-smelling spices for his burial. But on the Sabbath they rested, as the Law of Moses commands.

Luke 23.44–56

UNDERSTANDING THE TEXT

1. Jesus' last words were spoken to his "Father." Look at the first words that Jesus speaks in Luke's gospel (page 39). Why do you think that Luke draws similarities between Jesus' first and last words?

2. Look in the passage for everything that shows the day and time and write up a schedule of the events.

3. Look for individuals and groups of people. What are their different reactions as they are faced with Jesus' death?

CHAPTER 35
DEATH
AND THE TOMB

CRYING OUT

We cry when our hearts and bodies are hurting, when we are sad or feel lost. We cry out so the anguish and pain inside of us will come out, so someone may hear us and come to help us. A cry is a call for help. When we cry out to people who love, we trust they will answer. We are sure — when they hear our cry they will come to relieve our suffering. There is also a sort of joy. As if Jesus was saying to God, "God, thanks to your love, I was able to hold out. I went all the way in my mission." Crosses and death don't have the power to stop someone who trusts in God.

CHANGING AND BELIEVING

When the Roman officer saw Jesus on the cross, he was "changed." Up to that point the officer had believed what he had heard about Jesus: rumors and slanderous remarks. Now, as he saw what was happening, the Roman officer was "turned around" — converted. He saw things in a new light. He finally discovered who Jesus was. He finally understood the meaning of what Jesus said and did. Some events influence our lives and transform our way of seeing Jesus and believing in him. When this happens we can understand that Jesus loves us and is always present. Then we can say, like the Roman officer, "I didn't know him! He is really our Lord. He 'changed' our lives! I believe in him!" If we believe in Jesus we let ourselves be "changed" and "converted" by him, and we according to his gospel.

DEATH

Life stops. We finish living, loving and creating. As if someone closed the curtain on us. But is life really over? What if the curtain opened onto a new future? Jesus dies, like us. He knows death. He accompanies us through this ordeal.

GRAVES

Graves remind us of mourning, of the loss of a loved one. They make us think of holes that swallow up life and joy. But don't graves also remind us of holes we dig in the ground to plant the seed that will blossom into a flower or a tree? When Jesus spoke about himself, didn't he say, "The seed must die in the ground in order to give life!" Jesus was laid in a grave like all human beings. As seeds when they are sown. This is why graves are places that give hope. Isn't that why we lay flowers there?

INTO YOUR HANDS

With you, Lord,
there is shelter!
You protect me
as a rock protects me
when winds threaten
to blow me down!

With you, Lord,
there is freedom!
You break the chains of evil
that imprison me.

With you, Lord,
there is light!
Your light fills my eyes
and my heart that once held fear.
I trust in you.
You save me.
You are my God!

With joy and trust
I offer my life to you.
My life will always be protected
in your care.
You surround my life with your love,
as we shelter a fragile flame
in our hands to protect it
from the storm.
You, Lord, carry my life
to the other side of death
— into new life in your Kingdom.

IN JESUS' DAY

WHEN THE GOSPELS WERE WRITTEN

The day after Jesus' death was terrible for his friends. It was the Sabbath day (Saturday). The sad images of the arrest, suffering and death of their master filled their hearts and minds. They had left everything for him. They had placed all their hope in him. Now everything was over. They felt like orphans.

The next morning (Sunday), the women who helped Jesus bought perfumed oil and went to the tomb to anoint the body that had been placed there in haste. They had been the last ones to leave the cross. They were the first ones to go back to the tomb.

When they arrived, they were shocked. The stone that had blocked the entrance to the tomb had been rolled aside. Jesus' body had disappeared. Where was it? Had it been stolen or laid somewhere else? Who had done this? Were these the actions of a friend or an enemy? What happened during the night? They would soon understand that Jesus was alive, but for the moment they didn't see him. They felt that they were faced with something that was beyond their understanding. They ran away, filled with great fear.

Peter and John went to make sure things were as the women said. It was true: Jesus wasn't there anymore! The women were right!

Little by little Jesus' friends understood that he was alive. Many said they had seen him. Later Paul states that the Lord appeared to many: "Christ appeared to Peter, then to the twelve. After this, he appeared to more than five hundred other followers... He also appeared to James, and then to all of the apostles. Finally, he appeared to me" (1 Corinthians 15.4-8).

The disciples experienced Jesus in a different way. They proclaimed throughout the world that he was alive, that God had raised him, that he woke from among the dead, that he got up, that he was risen.

Later, the authors of the gospels told the story of Jesus' life. They all gave a lot of details about his suffering and death. They also spoke about what happened on Passover night. It had been possible to see and describe the suffering. But for the resurrection, it was only possible to have faith and spread the Good News.

This day after the Sabbath, the first day of the week, became known to Christians as "the Lord's Day," Sunday, a celebration of the resurrected Jesus.

THE RESURRECTION

THE GOSPEL

¹ After the Sabbath, Mary Magdalene, Salome, and Mary the mother of James bought some spices to put on Jesus' body. ² Very early on Sunday morning, just as the sun was coming up, they went to the tomb. ³ On their way, they were asking one another, "Who will roll the stone away from the entrance for us?" ⁴ But when they looked, they saw that the stone had

...lready been rolled away. And it was a huge ...tone!

The women went into the tomb, and on the ...ight side they saw a young man in a white ...obe sitting there. They were alarmed.

The man said, "Don't be alarmed! You are ...ooking for Jesus from Nazareth, who was ...ailed to a cross. God has raised him to life, ...nd he isn't here. You can see the place ...here they put his body. [7] Now go and tell his ...isciples, and especially Peter, that he will ...o ahead of you to Galilee. You will see him ...here, just as he told you."

When the women ran from the tomb, they ...ere confused and shaking all over. They ...ere too afraid to tell anyone what had hap...ened.

Mark 16.1–8

UNDERSTANDING THE TEXT

1. Why were the women going to the tomb?

2. Why was the man dressed in white there?

3. Look up the meaning of the following words in the glossary: *white* and *resurrection*.

4. Look in the introduction to see how the events that follow Jesus' death are retold (page 15).

5. Look for words that express darkness and light in the passage about Jesus' death (pages 198 and 199) and in this passage.

THE RESURRECTION

LIVING TODAY

Night

Hope is broken. Friends are gone. Sadness fills our hearts. Death is at the door. We don't know where to turn. We have lost our way and can't trust, not even God. We feel surrounded by a darkness full of shadows. We don't dare to look for the way out. It is night! For Jesus' friends, it was night.

Day

There is a little sliver of light on the horizon. So small! Little more than a glimmer of light. So fragile! But night has broken. Slowly the light grows stronger and advances, chasing the shadows away. Finally the light is all around; it lights up faces and hearts. Day has broken! That morning, day broke upon the disciples.

Risen

God raised Jesus from the grave. He is risen! All the forces that had gathered against him — hate, exclusion, lies and evil — are defeated. Jesus' love and trust in God have conquered them all! Even death has lost its power. When Jesus Christ arose he took away death's power. Jesus is the Lord of life. Jesus crossed the barrier between death and life — opened the way between the two. This opening will never close. The risen Jesus walks ahead of us, removing obstacles that stand in the way. From now on, hope is found in death! When we follow in Jesus' footsteps, we go to the other side of death — to life.

Sunday

Thanks to Jesus who rose from the dead, Easter is the first day of a new world where life triumphs. Every Sunday is like an Easter celebration that helps us enter little by little into the joy of the risen Christ. On Sunday Christians get together and marvel at everything Jesus did through his life and death. Then throughout the week they work with him against all the forces of death — within themselves and in the world. Believing in the risen Christ means chasing away the darkness and night in the world and spreading daylight by living according to Jesus' gospel.

LIVING

Let us all sing,
"Alleluia and thank you!"
Because Jesus our Lord is standing
— risen and alive.
Death could not hold him!
Death was defeated!

Jesus came to this earth
to bring God's Good News
of forgiveness and peace
to everyone.

On the cross he carried
all the heavy burdens of our lives.
On the cross he opened his arms
to share the treasures
found in God's love.
He spread life along the way.

Evil rose up against Jesus.
Hate tried to stop him.
Cruelty schemed to make him fall.
And even death sharpened
its sword to defeat him
and drag him into the tomb.
But they lost.

Because God raised Jesus.

Come, friends, praise God
and sing, "Alleluia and joy!
Thank you, Lord of life,
for defeating death!
Here we stand, ready to follow you
into your new life!
Alleluia and thank you,
Jesus Christ,
our Lord and our God!"

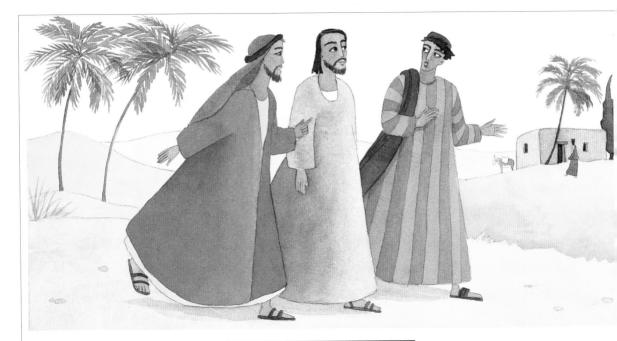

THE DISCIPLES FROM EMMAUS

IN JESUS' DAY

After Jesus' death some of his friends were discouraged. Others got together and continued to hope. Soon they discovered that the living Jesus was always with them. But sometimes they didn't recognize him.

WHEN THE GOSPELS WERE WRITTEN

After many years Luke described what happened on Easter night: two discouraged disciples met, welcomed, recognized and then told others of the living Jesus. Luke wrote this for Christians who weren't able to discover that Jesus was present in their lives. He showed them that they can find him — like the discouraged disciples did — when they welcome strangers, when they talk and listen heart-to-heart, when they are hospitable, when they read the Bible, when they pray and when they share what they have.

THE GOSPEL

13 That same day two of Jesus' disciples were going to the village of Emmaus, which was about seven miles from Jerusalem. 14 As they were talking and thinking about what had happened, 15 Jesus came near and started walking along beside them. 16 But they did not know who he was.

17 Jesus asked them, "What were you talking about as you walked along?"

The two of them stood there looking sad and gloomy. 18 Then the one named Cleopas asked Jesus, "Are you the only person from Jerusalem who didn't know what was happening there these last few days?"

19 "What do you mean?" Jesus asked.

They answered:

Those things that happened to Jesus from Nazareth. By what he did and said he showed that he was a powerful prophet, who pleased God and all the people. ²⁰ Then the chief priests and our leaders had him arrested and sentenced to die on a cross. ²¹ We had hoped that he would be the one to set Israel free! But it has already been three days since all this happened.

²² Some women in our group surprised us. They had gone to the tomb early in the morning, ²³ but did not find the body of Jesus. They came back, saying that they had seen a vision of angels who told them that he is alive. ²⁴ Some men from our group went to the tomb and found it just as the women had said. But they didn't see Jesus either.

²⁵ Then Jesus asked the two disciples, "Why can't you understand? How can you be so slow to believe all that the prophets said? ²⁶ Didn't you know that the Messiah would have to suffer before he was given his glory?" ²⁷ Jesus then explained everything written about himself in the Scriptures, beginning with the Law of Moses and the Books of the Prophets.

²⁸ When the two of them came near the village where they were going, Jesus seemed to be going farther. ²⁹ They begged him, "Stay with us! It's already late, and the sun is going down." So Jesus went into the house to stay with them.

³⁰ After Jesus sat down to eat, he took some bread. He blessed it and broke it. Then he gave it to them. ³¹ At once they knew who he was, but he disappeared. ³² They said to each other, "When he talked with us along the road and explained the Scriptures to us, didn't it warm our hearts?" ³³ So they got right up and returned to Jerusalem.

The two disciples found the eleven apostles and the others gathered together. ³⁴ And they learned from the group that the Lord was really alive and had appeared to Peter. ³⁵ Then the disciples from Emmaus told what happened on the road and how they knew he was the Lord when he broke the bread.

Luke 24.13-35

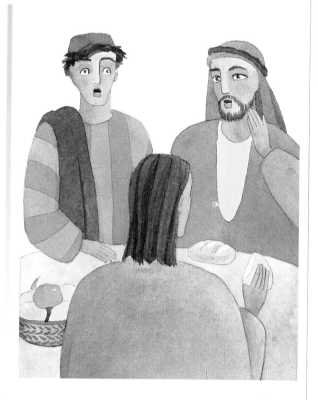

UNDERSTANDING THE TEXT

1. Reread the passage and look for all the things that helped the two men discover that Jesus was alive:
   - the actions
   - the words
   - the writings.

2. Look up the meanings of the following words in the glossary: *angel, scripture, breaking the bread, glory, Moses* and *prophets.*

LIVING
TODAY

DISCOURAGED

Sometimes in life we get discouraged because we have lost our faith in God. Because we feel that God has abandoned us. We feel sad. We think that we have lost God's love forever and that we are alone, without God's help or friendship. So we go on, dragging our feet, without hope, saying to ourselves, "What good is this?" In some ways it is as if we are dead.

SIGNS THAT GIVE LIFE

People with open hearts and living faith see signs of the living Christ. Even if they don't see him with their own eyes, they will discover that Jesus is present in their lives. Jesus' love is present in the forgiving word, given freely; his tenderness in the respect offered to an outcast and in the refusal to think badly of someone. Others recognize Jesus' peace when people try to get along and understand one another. They see Jesus' mercy as he gives himself so there can be more happiness in the world. The risen Jesus is seen in Christians acting according to the gospel and in Christians gathering at church.

These "signs" give us hope! We are happy because we know that the living Jesus is walking with us on the road of life.

THE TABLE OF THE LORD

The Lord Jesus left a sign by which his friends could recognize him: the breaking of the bread! The disciples had seen Jesus breaking bread and giving thanks to God the Father so often before each meal when he was among them! This is how they suddenly realized that the stranger they listened to so carefully was Jesus himself. In the same way Jesus invites us to the table where the Living Word of God is present among his friends. In the Gospel, proclaimed and received, Jesus invites every Christian to trust him and to walk with him through life. Jesus breaks the bread and pours the wine and offers to share his love with everyone. Every time that Christians celebrate the Lord's Supper, they are therefore called to recognize Jesus in their midst and go forth to spread the news that Jesus Christ is among the living, supporting them and encouraging them as they walk toward unending joy.

ON THE ROAD

*Stay with us, Lord,
as night approaches
and evil hunts and tries to trap us.
May your presence
light our path, Lord!*

*Walk with us, Lord,
as night falls
and our strength wavers
before the work that is still at hand.
Sustain us
with the bread of your presence!*

*Show us the way, Lord,
when our hearts are blind
and we do not see the signs
that you give us every day!
Come with us, Lord,
and let your presence
shine in our lives!*

ON THE LAKE SHORE

IN JESUS' DAY

Some of Jesus' friends went home. Others decided to stay together for a while in Jerusalem. At some point those from Galilee decided to go back to their region. Peter, Thomas, Nathanael, James and John returned to their work as fishermen on Lake Tiberias.

At the same time they were discovering the Risen One and how to live with him. It wasn't always easy. Mary Magdalene mistook him for a gardener. The disciples from Emmaus walked a long way with him before they recognized him. By the lake, Peter and his companions knew that it was the Lord who was inviting them to eat. Nonetheless, they were afraid to ask, "Who are you?"

They understood more and more that the Bible spoke of a Messiah that had to suffer, be put to death and rise again. They also realized that the living Lord wasn't just a corpse that had been given the same life as before. Such a person would have to die again. They discovered that Jesus was totally transformed. His body was "already in glory," similar to the body he had when he was transfigured on the mountain in front of his disciples. But it was truly Jesus. To recognize Jesus, it wasn't enough to "see;" you also had to believe.

WHEN THE GOSPELS WERE WRITTEN

At the end of John's gospel there is a story about Jesus appearing on the shores of Lake Tiberias.

The author wasn't just telling a story. John wanted to show readers how they, too, could find the Risen One.

- There is no need to travel a great distance. Jesus could be found in everyday life. Peter and his friends were working when Jesus joined them.
- We all need God's love. "Jesus' favorite" disciple recognized him first not Peter, who was the leader of the group.
- We have to help each other. Peter and his companions worked together. John said to Peter, "It is the Lord."
- We have to remember Jesus' meals. On this same lake, the disciples had caught a miraculous number of fish with Jesus. He had shared meals of bread and fish with them many times.

The author also wants to suggest something else. Jesus had said to his disciples, "I will make you fishers of men and women." The account can have a hidden, symbolic meaning; the fish represent the many people who listened to the disciples and became Christians.

CHAPTER 38
ON THE LAKE SHORE

THE GOSPEL

[1] Jesus later appeared to his disciples along the shore of Lake Tiberias. [2] Simon Peter, Thomas the Twin, Nathanael from Cana in Galilee, and the brothers James and John, were there, together with two other disciples. [3] Simon Peter said, "I'm going fishing!"

The others said, "We will go with you." They went out in their boat. But they didn't catch a thing that night.

[4] Early the next morning Jesus stood on the shore, but the disciples did not realize who he was. [5] Jesus shouted, "Friends, have you caught anything?"

"No!" they answered.

[6] So he told them, "Let your net down on the right side of your boat, and you will catch some fish."

They did, and the net was so full of fish that they could not drag it up into the boat.

[7] Jesus' favorite disciple told Peter, "It's the Lord!" When Simon heard that it was the Lord, he put on the clothes that he had taken off while he was working. Then he jumped into the water. [8] The boat was only about a hundred yards from shore. So the other disciples stayed in the boat and dragged in the net full of fish.

[9] When the disciples got out of the boat, they saw some bread and a charcoal fire with fish on it. [10] Jesus told his disciples, "Bring some of the fish you just caught." [11] Simon Peter got back into the boat and dragged the net to shore. In it were one hundred fifty-three large fish, but still the net did not rip.

[12] Jesus said, "Come and eat!" But none of the disciples dared ask who he was. They knew he was the Lord. [13] Jesus took the bread in his hands and gave some of it to his disciples. He did the same with the fish. [14] This was the third time that Jesus appeared to his disciples after he was raised from death.

John 21.1-14

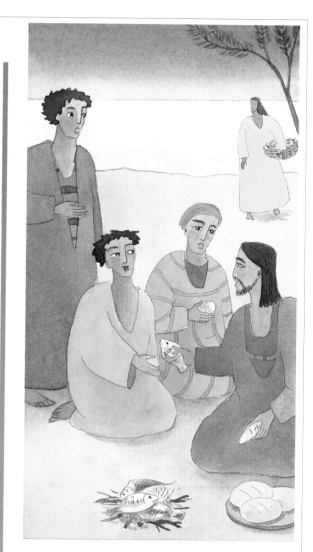

UNDERSTANDING THE TEXT

1. Look for deeds from Jesus' life found in this passage:
- sharing bread and fish (page 113)
- the call to become fishers of men and women (page 53)
- another miraculous catch.

2. On the map and the glossary look for Galilee and the town of Cana where Nathanael was born. What else happened in this village?

LIVING TODAY

Every day

To meet the risen Lord there is no need to travel very far, to run away to a dark room, or to get away from everyone. On the contrary — Jesus can be found every day in everything in our daily lives. We find Jesus in the classrooms and in the hallways of our schools, among the many different faces. We see Jesus in hospital rooms whenever comfort is given; wherever people try to transform the world. We meet Jesus in organizations that work to improve the living conditions of other people; among Christians who gather in Jesus' name and who act out of love for their neighbor. We see the risen Lord everywhere men and women, young and old, live. Jesus, the Living Lord, helps all to grow in God's image every day. Jesus helps us all rise again to new life!

Together

If we are not shown the way we may not pay any attention to the risen Lord who is with us everyday! Our hearts and minds have to be open. Over time our hope in Jesus can become smothered by worries and needs, like a fire that is put out by wet leaves. We help one another see — "The Lord is here!" We sharpen our alertness so that we can recognize Jesus better. We remember what Jesus did and said; we reflect and pray. We support those who would like to give up, thinking that Jesus is not present, here or anywhere. We show them where Jesus can be found — "Look there! Look hard!" We are witnesses to the risen Lord. We spread the Good News!

Look – listen

Jesus lives in us every day. When Jesus' love lives in our heart, it is easy for us to recognize him. Jesus' love grows when we are filled with love. How can we love Jesus? All we have to do is watch him and listen! Look at Jesus raising the paralyzed man, touching the leper, laughing with the children and offering his life on the cross. Listen to Jesus forgiving the adulterous woman, encouraging Zacchaeus to change his way of life, announcing happiness by the Beatitudes and giving his Spirit.
As we get to know Jesus and all that he did, our faith gets stronger. We recognize him on the "shores of our lake"; we see him in our daily lives.

SO MANY PLACES

There are so many people
to get to know,
so much work left to finish,
so much of the Gospel to discover,
so many prayers
and silent moments,
so many projects to begin
and complete
for the good of everyone.

So many places
where we can meet you
in faith and love!

But you know us, Lord!
Our attention is divided
in so many ways!
But you are there
in so many different places.
You meet us in all that we do.
You do not let us forget
the sound of your Word.

Show yourself, Lord.
Show yourself so we can recognize
you at the four corners
of the world each day.
So we can cry with joy,
"It is you, Lord!"

CHAPTER 39

THE ASCENSION

IN JESUS' DAY

For a while Jesus' friends experienced the reappearances of their risen Lord. But this didn't last forever. After his reappearances came separation, absence and the long wait for his return.

The disciples had a hard time letting go of their old ideas — they continued to wonder if, someday, Jesus was going to reestablish the kingdom of Israel, to overthrow the Romans and put his friends in good positions. They needed to understand that the strength Jesus gave them was not that of an army, but that of the Spirit. The Spirit would help them become witnesses to Jesus' love.

The disciples knew that, though Jesus had gone, their mission was just beginning. They had to accept this reality. The disciples couldn't just stand there staring at the sky. They were sent to proclaim what they experienced. Jerusalem became the starting point for the disciples' mission that would lead them to the ends of the earth.

WHEN THE GOSPELS WERE WRITTEN

Luke wrote two books: a gospel and the Acts of the Apostles. Luke's gospel ends with *"Jesus left and was taken up to heaven"* (Luke 24.51). The Acts of the Apostles starts with the story of Jesus going to heaven (Acts 1.6-11). In the gospel, Jesus is present physically. In Acts, he is no longer present physically; he acts through his Spirit.

The mystery of the Risen One is expressed in many ways in the Christian Scriptures: he is living, he woke up, he rose. Luke also wanted to show us that Jesus was "glorified" by God; he entered into God's glory.

The people in Jesus' day thought that the earth was flat and that heaven was overhead. God lived in this mysterious sky. It was quite normal for Luke to describe Jesus' entry into God's glory as Jesus being raised up into the sky.

Luke is also the only author of the gospel to link important Jewish celebrations with the disciples' experience of the risen Lord. Jesus appeared to them over the course of forty days (Acts 1.3). Then he was lifted up before their eyes. He sent them his Spirit on the day of Pentecost, ten days later (fifty days after Easter).

Luke wanted to help Christians remember these important events in the years following Jesus' death and resurrection:
- Jewish Passover (commemorating the liberation from Egypt) provides the underpinnings for and shapes the celebration of the Resurrection;
- the forty days (a sacred time) until the Ascension allowed for the remembering of the presence of the risen Lord;
- the fiftieth day, Pentecost (the Jewish harvest celebration), became the celebration of the gift of the Holy Spirit.

THE ACTS
OF THE APOSTLES

[6] While the apostles were still with Jesus, they asked him, "Lord, are you now going to give Israel its own king again?"

[7] Jesus said to them, "You don't need to know the time of those events that only the Father controls. [8] But the Holy Spirit will come upon you and give you power. Then you will tell everyone about me in Jerusalem, in all Judea, in Samaria, and everywhere in the world." [9] After Jesus had said this and while they were watching, he was taken up into a cloud. They could not see him, [10] but as he went up, they kept looking up into the sky.

Suddenly two men dressed in white clothes were standing there beside them. [11] They said, "Why are you men from Galilee standing here and looking up into the sky? Jesus has been taken to heaven. But he will come back in the same way that you have seen him go."

Acts 1.6-11

UNDERSTANDING THE TEXT

1. In this passage, Luke talks about God the Father, Jesus the Son, and the Holy Spirit.
Look for what it says about each of these characters.

2. This passage speaks of messengers who help people understand the meaning of what happened.
Do you know other messengers?
Look on page 31 and page 205.

3. Look up the meanings of the following words in the glossary: *cloud, heaven, white* and *forty.*

THE ASCENSION

LIVING TODAY

ON THE EARTH

You don't become a disciple of Jesus by seeking refuge near God as you might near a warm fire. Or by ignoring the needs of other people because you are thinking only of God. Or in avoiding the evil in this world because you don't want to get involved. We must be involved in the world and the lives of people! That is where Jesus Christ was born, lived, died and rose again. The road to God leads through this world of ours.

WITNESSES

With Jesus gone, the disciples became responsible for his mission. They had to show God's love and God's beauty to the world. To them, and to all who believe in him, Jesus Christ gives the great responsibility of bearing his message of love. It was their responsibility to proclaim what they saw and heard of the Son of God to others in this world. Their role was to be "witnesses." From now on the Good News is given to their hearts, mouths and hands. It is up to them to spread the Word! Being a witness is a full-time job, not simply a title! Being a Christian witness is very important because it is important to plant the seed of happiness and new life everywhere. The word "Christian" comes from "Christ." Aren't Christians Christ-like, empowered by Christ's Spirit to spread his love to all living creatures? Even if this means giving up everything that they own and are?

CELEBRATING FEAST DAYS

Being a witness: what a wonderful but difficult task! Witnesses have to keep renewing their faith. That's why they need to celebrate, with the People of God, special days that commemorate Christ's acts and words. Not just to sit around and recall good memories, but to realize that Jesus Christ continues to free and to love today's world. Each time we celebrate, it is as if Christians had returned to the source — Jesus comes to show his love and joy as he opens God's house to all the children of the world. Each time the Holy Spirit makes Christians better witnesses!

LORD

Greater than leprosy
that wears out body and heart,
greater than scorn
that judges without pity,
greater than sin
that takes control of us,
your love is wider
than the sky and the earth,
Jesus, Christ, Lord!

Greater than selfishness
that makes us want to keep
everything for ourselves,
greater than hate
that nails the living to a cross,
greater than death
that makes the living fearful,
your life is stronger
than the night and the tomb,
Jesus, Christ, Lord!

Your friends are gathered here
with joy to help those who long
for justice, to share with the needy,
to spread mercy,
to lift up those who are afflicted,
to establish truth, to build a world
of peace and tenderness!

Here we are, Jesus, Christ, Lord,
to proclaim your Word in our cities
and homes and to all the children
of the world!

CHAPTER 40

PENTECOST

IN JESUS' DAY

Jerusalem was the religious center of the Jewish people. But Jews didn't live just in Palestine. They were spread throughout the many countries around the Mediterranean Sea and as far as India and southern Egypt.

Some Jews, the very pious and rich, traveled to spend their last days in Jerusalem. Others came on pilgrimages for feast days. At Passover they celebrated the beginning of the harvest and commemorated their ancestors' liberation from slavery in Egypt. At "Pentecost" they celebrated the end of the harvest and commemorated the day God gave the law to Moses on Mount Sinai. A very diverse crowd filled the streets of Jerusalem at these times.

Jesus made it very clear to his disciples that it was important to carry on his mission after he was gone. It wouldn't be easy. But Jesus promised he would give his friends the strength of his Spirit. There are fifty days between Easter (which follows Jesus' death) and Pentecost. Seven weeks during which the disciples and their friends could gather their thoughts and feelings. They didn't give up. With the strength of the Spirit they were able to go to the ends of the earth.

WHEN THE GOSPELS WERE WRITTEN

The story of Pentecost isn't told in the gospels but is found in Luke's second book, the Acts of the Apostles. Luke describes how those who followed Jesus continued working in Jerusalem, in Palestine, and to the ends of the earth. Luke is certain that it is Jesus' Spirit that gave them this strength. This Spirit is like a wind that penetrates every nook and cranny, like a fire that warms hearts, or like a power that breaks down barriers of race and language.

When Luke wrote, a few decades after Jesus' death, the disciples — some of whom spoke Aramaic with a strong Galilean accent — had managed to travel throughout the known world. Pentecost was the beginning of this "explosion" that unites all men and women.

THE ACTS
OF THE
APOSTLES

¹ On the day of Pentecost all the Lord's followers were together in one place. ² Suddenly there was a noise from heaven like the sound of a mighty wind! It filled the house where they were meeting. ³ Then they saw what looked like fiery tongues moving in all directions, and a tongue came and settled on each person there. ⁴ The Holy Spirit took control of everyone, and they began speaking whatever languages the Spirit let them speak.

⁵ Many religious Jews from every country in the world were living in Jerusalem. ⁶ And when they heard this noise, a crowd gathered. But they were surprised, because they were hearing everything in their own languages. ⁷ They were excited and amazed, and said:

Don't all these who are speaking come from Galilee? [8] Then why do we hear them speaking our very own languages? [9] Some of us are from Parthia, Media, and Elam. Others are from Mesopotamia, Judea, Cappadocia, Pontus, Asia, [10] Phrygia, Pamphylia, Egypt, parts of Libya near Cyrene, Rome, [11] Crete, and Arabia. Some of us were born Jews, and others of us have chosen to be Jews. Yet we all hear them using our own languages to tell the wonderful things God has done.

[12] Everyone was excited and confused. Some of them even kept asking each other, "What does all this mean?"

[13] Others made fun of the Lord's followers and said, "They are drunk."

[14] Peter stood with the eleven apostles and spoke in a loud and clear voice to the crowd:

Friends and everyone else living in Jerusalem, listen carefully to what I have to say! [15] You are wrong to think that these people are drunk. After all, it is only nine o'clock in the morning. [16] But this is what God had the prophet Joel say,

[17] "When the last days come,
 I will give my Spirit
     to everyone..."

Acts 2.1-17

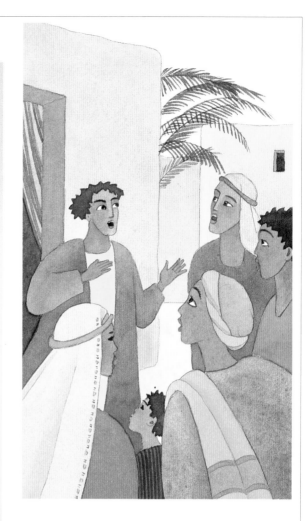

UNDERSTANDING THE TEXT

1. Look at the map and try to find the countries of all the different people who were gathered in Jerusalem for Pentecost.

2. What are the different interpretations given to the events described in this passage? Look at the second-last paragraph.

3. Do you know of other passages in the Bible where the images of wind and fire are used to show God's presence?

LIVING
TODAY

HOLY SPIRIT

How can we continue Jesus' work when we are people whose faith is fragile and who even deny Jesus in hard times? We need Christ's Spirit in order to accomplish our mission. The gift of the Spirit fills us. We receive it when we accept by faith that Jesus is our Savior and Lord. With our hearts and minds the Spirit helps us enter into the mystery of our Lord Jesus. As the sun that spreads its warmth, the infinite love of God shines in us and makes us understand that we are God's beloved children. It inspires us to follow the gospel. As the wind helps the sailboat skim along the crest of the waves, the Spirit sets us in motion on the path shown to us by Jesus. The Spirit sweeps away our fear and is the source of our desire to become Christians. It inspires us to make Christ's Good News visible in our words and actions.

NO MORE BARRIERS

So many barriers separate human beings: poverty, misunderstanding, riches, pride, color of skin, language, religion, prejudice, cultures. These divisions make us see each other as rivals whom we cannot trust, or enemies whom we must defeat. These are the results of hearts full of hurt and fear!
The Holy Spirit destroys these barriers and divisions. A new world begins with the Spirit. With the Spirit, people are no longer rivals but brothers and sisters, called to love each other with respect and understanding. God's love takes shape when we let the Spirit work in us. God's love unites us all in a single family where everyone can experience God's love.

THE CHURCH

All who are open to God's love, who live Christ's gospel and are guided by the Holy Spirit, make up the Church. The Church has spread throughout the entire world. Its mission is to make Christ's Word heard everywhere so that it can be accepted by those who are waiting for the Good News. All the children of the world must have access to God's marvels through the actions and members of the Church. The Holy Spirit dwells within the Church to help her remain holy so that God's infinite tenderness can be seen and touched. Friends, we are the Church!

COME!

A PRAYER FOR TODAY

Come, Holy Spirit!
Give us gentleness
so we can reach out to others
instead of judging and condemning!

Come, Holy Spirit!
Give us joy
so we can share it with those
who have lost hope!

Come, Holy Spirit!
Give us trust
so we can stand strong amidst fear,
and know that God
is our faithful friend!

Come, Holy Spirit!
Give us peace
so we can build bridges
that allow people
to be together!

Come, Spirit of God!
Give us strength
so we can live like Jesus Christ!

Come, Spirit of God!
Give us the desire to live
with our hearts and minds open
to the sunshine of Jesus' Word!

Come, Holy Spirit!
Come to our world!
Blow the Good News
of Jesus Christ
into the lives of all people!

JERUSALEM IN JESUS' TIME

In the distance, the Jordan Valley

The Western (or Wailing) Wall Today

In the distance, the Dead Sea

The Mount of Olives

The Temple

Antonia Fortress

The Garden of Gethsemane

Bethany

Bethphage

Golgotha

The Kidron Valley

Jesus' Tomb

Herod's Palace
Pilate's Residence

The House of Caiaphas

The Site of the Last Supper

The Pool of Siloam

Glossary

GLOSSARY

A

ABBA
A word in Aramaic, the language spoken by Jesus, meaning, "Oh father, my father" or even "Daddy." Jesus used this word to address God (Mark 14.36). Christians can also pray, "Abba! Father!" (Romans 8.15).

ABRAHAM
The leader of a tribe of nomads in the 19th century B.C. He is seen as the ancestor of the people of the Bible. He later came to be known as the father of Jewish and Christian believers. From Jesus' time on, all people are called to become "sons and daughters of Abraham."

ADORE
Today this word most often means "to love very much." In the Bible, to adore was to pray to or to worship someone — God, the emperor or another. Jesus is clear about this: "The Scriptures say, 'Worship the Lord your God and serve only him'" (Matthew 4.10).

AGREEMENT
See COVENANT.

AMEN
Hebrew word meaning "in truth" or "really." In the gospels it often means that the author is calling for the audience's attention. Today it is an acclamation used to end prayers.

ANDREW
A fisherman who lived in Capernaum. He and Simon Peter were among Jesus' first apostles.

ANGEL
In the Bible angels are seen as God's messengers. They make God's will known. The angel Gabriel announced to Mary that she would be Jesus' mother (Luke 1.26-38). Today, even if we don't see angels, we can still discover what God asks of us by reading the Bible, praying and meditating, paying attention to others and being aware of what is going on in the world.

ANOINTING
The action of applying oil, especially as a sacred ritual. This gesture often has a religious meaning. Kings were anointed at their coronation. Some prophets or high priests were consecrated by the sign of anointing. The word *Messiah* means "he who was anointed." See CHRIST.

APOSTLE
This word means "one who is sent." In the gospels the twelve

apostles were called and sent by Jesus. Later, apostles were those who were sent by the churches to proclaim the Good News. Paul was the "Apostle to the Nations." Today, every Christian is called to be an apostle.

B

BAPTISM
In Greek, the word *baptize* means to immerse or plunge into water. Water washes. It purifies. In Jesus' day people were baptized by John the Baptist. This purification of the body signified that they were converted. Jesus spoke of baptism in water and in the Spirit. For Christians, baptism means being united with Jesus Christ and belonging to Christ's Church.

BEATITUDE
A phrase often found in the Bible, beginning with "God blesses." It announces happiness for those who live in God's way. Matthew and Luke report the Beatitudes proclaimed by Jesus, e.g., "God blesses those people who depend only on him" (Matthew 5.3; Luke 6.20).

BETHLEHEM
In Hebrew — the house *(beth)* of bread *(lehem)*. A town located four miles south of Jerusalem in the hills of Judea. Birthplace of King David (around 1035 B.C.). According to Matthew, Luke and John, Jesus was born in Bethlehem.

BLASPHEMY
Blasphemy is the act of saying words or doing things that demonstrate a bold irreverence toward God. According to Matthew, Jesus was condemned because his accusers claimed that he blasphemed when he said that he would sit "at the right side of God" (Matthew 26.64-66).

BREAKING THE BREAD
An action often done by the head of the family, breaking and sharing the bread with the family. Jesus broke the bread to feed the crowd that followed him. On the eve of his death, to commemorate the Passover and knowing that his death was near, Jesus "blessed the bread and broke it. Then he gave it to his disciples and said, 'Take this and eat it. This is my body'" (Matthew 26.26). The early Christians gathered together to break bread (Acts 20.7).

C

CANA
A town in Galilee on the road from Nazareth to Tiberias. According to John, Jesus performed his first miracle here when he changed water into wine during a wedding celebration (John 2.1-11).

CAPERNAUM
One of the many settlements on the shores of Lake Tiberias. A border town with a customs office and Roman soldiers. Peter's mother-in-law lived in this fishing town. Jesus went to Capernaum; he healed the sick there. For a while it was his center of activity.

CHIEF PRIESTS
These were priests from the Temple with important responsibilities: the High Priest, the former High Priests, the Temple police chiefs, the Temple treasurers, the leaders of groups of priests. They had a great influence over the Sanhedrin (the High Council). They were angry with Jesus because he questioned their authority.

CHRIST
The Israelites were waiting for a Savior who was promised by God

— the Messiah (in Hebrew) or the Christ (in Greek). When Jesus' disciples recognized him as the promised Savior, they called him "Jesus the Christ." Very soon, "the" was dropped and he was called "Jesus Christ."

CHRISTIAN

Christians are those who follow Christ. They practice what Jesus taught. When the gospels were written there was a distinction made between Christians who had converted from Judaism and those who came directly from the non-Jewish, or pagan, world. They had to learn to live together and to respect their differences.

CIRCUMCISION

Circumcision is the removal of the foreskin of a male child. For Jews this ritual was a sign of the agreement that God made with Israel (called the Covenant). Jesus was circumcised eight days after his birth (Luke 2.21). When many pagans began to convert to Christianity, Paul argued that they shouldn't have to be circumcised. He won his case during the assembly of Jerusalem in the year 49 A.D. (Acts 15.1–35).

CLEAN/UNCLEAN

See PURE/IMPURE.

CLOUD

In biblical imagery clouds both reveal and hide the presence of God. Reference to a cloud in scripture indicates that God is present, though unseen; so God's mystery remains hidden. Clouds are found in the stories of Jesus' transfiguration (Mark 9.2-10) and ascension (Acts 1.6-11).

CONVERSION

To convert means two things. First, it means to change direction, to turn around, to come back toward God and others. Second, it means changing how we think — to repent and to change our hearts. In keeping with the prophets, John the Baptist, Jesus, and the disciples called men and women to "stop sinning and turn to God" (Acts 26.20).

COVENANT (AGREEMENT)

Throughout the Bible this word refers to the strong ties of faithful love that bind God and the people. The sign of the covenant (or agreement) was the blood of animals that had been sacrificed. This was replaced by the blood of Jesus. This is God's new covenant with humanity (Matthew 26.28). The books of the First Covenant are found in the Hebrew Scriptures.

D

DAVID

The greatest king of Israel. Born in Bethlehem, he reigned from 1004 B.C. to 965 B.C. The people's memory of him remained very vivid throughout the Bible. When times were hard, people dreamed of a new kingdom of David. During the Roman occupation many people thought of Jesus as the "son of David." Matthew's gospel tells us that Jesus is, in fact, a descendant of David (Matthew 1.6, 16, 17).

"DEACON"

A Greek word meaning "one who serves." Seven "deacons" were chosen by the twelve apostles to help them support the poor and care for the sick (Acts 6.1-7). We know the name of two of them: Stephen, the first Christian martyr (Acts 7.2-53) and Philip, who proclaimed the Good News in Samaria and Ethiopia (Acts 8.26-40).

DEMON

In ancient times demons were seen as spirits who influenced peoples' lives. In Jesus' day demons were evil spirits who opposed God. The devil was considered to be the leader of the demons (Matthew 25.41). The gospels present Jesus as being stronger than demons. He commanded them to be quiet. He made them leave people who were possessed (Mark 1.23-27). See SATAN.

DESERT

The desert is a dry, desolate place. Life is very difficult there. Palestine is surrounded by desert to the east and south. In the Bible, the desert is a place of testing. It is also a place to meet God as Moses and Elijah did. It was normal for Jesus to take time in the desert to reflect before starting on his mission (Matthew 4.1-11).

DEVIL

See DEMON or SATAN.

DIASPORA

Greek word meaning "dispersion." In Jesus' day, approximately four million Jews lived outside Palestine, spread throughout towns in the Roman Empire. They maintained close ties with Jerusalem. They read the Hebrew Scriptures. Paul preached first to those dispersed Jews during his travels.

DISCIPLE

A disciple is someone who studies with a rabbi or a master. John the Baptist, Jesus and Paul had disciples. The gospels speak of forty (or seventy-two) disciples, both men and women, who followed Jesus. Later, all those who tried to live like Jesus were considered to be disciples (Acts 6.1).

DONKEY

In ancient times, donkeys were often ridden. Later they were replaced during battles by horses. The Messiah, King of Peace, had to ride on a donkey (Zechariah 9.9). Jesus rode a donkey during his solemn entrance into Jerusalem. Many people were expecting a military Messiah who would end the Roman occupation (Mark 11.2).

DOVE

This was the only bird that could be offered as a sacrifice. Rich people offered sheep, goats or cows. The poor offered a pair of doves. Joseph and Mary offered doves after Jesus was born (Luke 2.24). The dove also has a figurative meaning. It represents the Spirit of God flying above the waters during the creation of the world. The gospels use this image to show that the Spirit came upon Jesus when he was baptized (Matthew 3.16).

DREAM

In biblical times, visions and dreams were a mysterious thing. People believed that they were ways for God to communicate with human beings, to reveal hidden things, to indicate the future, or to entrust someone with a mission.

E

EAGER ONE

See ZEALOT.

ELDER

In the Hebrew Scriptures, elders were older men. They held authority in clans or villages. In Jesus' day, they were the leaders of the Jewish community in the synagogue. In Jerusalem, they were on the High Council, the Sanhedrin. In the early Church, elders became leaders of the Christian communities.

ELIJAH

Name of a prophet, meaning "Yahweh is God." He lived in Israel during the 9th century B.C. He intervened to defend God's honor against idols (Baals) and to reestablish justice. He disappeared mysteriously, on a chariot of fire, according to biblical tradition. This is why — in Jesus' day — people were expecting his return. John the Baptist was thought to be a new Elijah. The gospels present Jesus in the company of Moses and Elijah at the time of the Transfiguration. They want to show that Jesus is a continuation of the same holy story (Mark 9.2-10).

ESSENES

Members of a Jewish religious movement. There were approximately four thousand Essenes. They lived together in villages or monasteries. In 1947, six hundred manuscripts were discovered in caves along the Dead Sea, in the library of the Essenian convent in Qumran. Essenes considered themselves to be the true Israel. They didn't agree with the priests from Jerusalem. They expected a final battle between the people of light and the people of darkness. They disappeared in 68 A.D. during the Jewish war.

F

FAITH

In Jesus' day, most people were believers. Jews believed that God created the world, that God freed the Israelite people from Egypt and that God was always ready to intervene. But when faced with Jesus, people were asked to go one step further. Accepting the Good News meant believing that the crucified Jesus was the Son of God who was raised from the dead. We need to discover God in the everyday events of our lives. Today, also, we are much freer to believe or to question, to doubt or to seek God. We discover that faith isn't an object that we possess, that can be thrown away or lost. Faith is a gift, a journey to be followed every day.

FESTIVAL OF THE THIN BREAD

Flat breads baked without yeast, that could be prepared quickly, reminded people of the food that was eaten in haste by the Hebrews right before their flight from Egypt. In Jesus' day the Festival of Thin Bread lasted one week, from the 15th to the 21st of Nisan (April). All the yeast was taken out of the house. Fermentation was seen as something inappropriate. The only type of bread that was eaten was unleavened bread. The Passover celebration took place at the beginning of this week, on the 15th of Nisan.

FIRE

Fire is fascinating and dangerous. It glows, warms, and purifies and cannot be captured. It can burn, destroy and consume. The Bible uses the image of fire in two ways: to represent destruction and punishment, and to suggest God's mystery. Moses discovered God in fire — in a burning bush. On Pentecost the Spirit's fire gave the disciples the strength to continue doing Jesus' work (Acts 2.1-13).

FORTY

In the Bible, the number forty often has a religious meaning. It means a sacred time, a time of walking toward God. Israel stayed for forty years in the desert before coming to the promised land. Elijah walked for forty days before he reached God's mountain. Jesus stayed for forty days in the desert before beginning his ministry.

G

GABRIEL

Meaning "God is my force." This name was given to the angel who appeared in the Christian Scriptures as God's messenger. He announced the births of John the Baptist (Luke 1.11-20) and of Jesus (Luke 1.26-38).

GALILEE

A region located in the northern part of Israel and east of Lake Tiberias having a pleasant climate. The people were lively and had a well-known accent. A fair distance from Jerusalem, the area was more in contact with neighboring nations. It was also a place where many rebellions against Rome originated. Jesus spent his early life in Galilee and also began his public life there.

GLORY

For us, glory means that someone is well known or famous. In the Bible, God's glory refers directly to God and is shown by God's action — in nature, in the history of the people and especially when God raised Jesus from the dead. Men and women can discover aspects of God's glory. They are called to participate in God's glory, now and in the future.

GOLD

Gold was used for jewelry, vases and decorations in the Temple and, much later, for making money. Gold was one of the gifts offered by the wise men to the infant Jesus. They gave him gold as they would to a king.

GOLGOTHA

Aramaic word meaning "skull." In Latin the word is "Calvary." A place outside the walls of Jerusalem used for executions of those condemned to death. It was near a cemetery. Jesus was crucified on Golgotha and laid in a tomb not far from there. Today the Church of the Holy Sepulcher stands on this place.

GOOD PEOPLE (RIGHTEOUS)

In the gospels, "good people" — we say "righteous" because they follow the right way of life — are contrasted with sinners. People are good, righteous, not because they observe the Law on the surface. They are righteous because they practice justice toward others and accept God's justice. God makes us good, righteous people.

GOSPEL

Word meaning "good news." In the Roman Empire the announcement of a victory or a celebration by the emperor was "good news," a gospel. In the Bible, the Good News is the announcement of salvation. God is coming to help humanity. God is coming to make people happy forever. Jesus proclaimed the Good News to the poor (Luke 4.13-30). The disciples were sent to proclaim the Gospel to all living creatures (Mark 16.15). Later, the four accounts that tell of the life, actions and words of Jesus were also called "gospels" — the gospels of Matthew, Mark, Luke and John.

GRACE (KINDNESS)

God's life in us. This is God's free gift, the expression of God's love. The fullness of God's grace — we also say "God's kindness" — is the gift of Jesus. Every woman and man is called to accept this gift and to draw life from it.

H

HEAVEN

When the Bible was written people thought that the earth was flat. The sky was overhead, this was where God lived. To respect God's name, people often spoke of "the heavens" instead of "God." The gospels speak of the Kingdom of Heaven and God's Kingdom.

HEROD

Member of a foreign royal family who, thanks to Rome, came into power in Jerusalem. Christian

Scriptures often speak of two people. Herod the Great, who reigned from 37 to 4 B.C., was cruel and bloodthirsty and had several of his family members executed. He was jealous of everyone and was despised. The gospels refer to him because of the Killing of the Children (Matthew 2.1-18). In order to get the Jews on his side, he ordered renovations to be made to the Temple structure. Herod Antipas, son of the first Herod, reigned in Galilee from 4 B.C. to 39 A.D. He had John the Baptist killed at the request of his mistress, Herodias (Matthew 14.3-13). Jesus called him a "fox" (Luke 13.32). He was in Jerusalem at the time of Jesus' trial, when Jesus was taken before him (Luke 23.8-12).

HIGH PRIEST

The most important person in the Jewish state. He was the leader of the people, at the head of the High Council (the Sanhedrin). He was the only person who could enter, once a year, the most secret part of the Temple, the place where God was thought to show himself: the Most Holy place. But in fact, the high priest was under the control of Rome. The emperor could name or dismiss him by taking away his vest-

ments, which were the signs of his responsibility. High priests often took advantage of their position. Families of candidates fought against one another. Sometimes the position of high priest came with financial compensation. The gospels speak of two high priests, Annas and Caiaphas, who played an important role in Jesus' condemnation.

HOLY SPIRIT

The Spirit is breath or wind. The Bible talks about God's Spirit who creates, who gives life. Christian Scriptures speak of the Holy Spirit working in Jesus' life, the lives of Christians and the life of the Church. The story of Pentecost describes in a solemn way how the Spirit began to act in the newborn Church (Acts 2.1-12).

HOSANNA (HOORAY!)

A very old Hebrew word used in prayers and praise. Hosanna, meaning "Come help us!" was also an exclamation of joy, like our "Hooray" (see Jesus' triumphal entry into Jerusalem, Matthew 21.9).

HOUR (TIME)

The day was divided into twelve hours between sunrise and sunset — 6:00 a.m. was the first hour;

9:00 a.m. was the third hour, etc. until 6:00 p.m. which was the twelfth. But the word "hour" also had a deeper meaning. It meant the moment that was chosen by God. The "hour" — or the "time" — of the Son of Man meant the time of his death and resurrection.

I

INCENSE

Precious resin imported from Arabia. It was used to make perfumed granules that were burned every day in the Temple in God's honor. Matthew notes that incense was among the gifts given to Jesus by the wise men (Matthew 2.11). Incense is a gift offered to God.

ISAIAH

A prophet of Jerusalem between 740 to 700 B.C. He was well known in the Temple and by the king. He was very close to God. The Book of Isaiah is essentially divided into two parts. It talks about the coming of a Messiah in great detail. This Messiah would be a suffering servant who would save the people of God from evil and sin. Jesus read a passage from the second part of this book in the synagogue of Nazareth (Luke 4), saying that the words of the prophet were now accomplished.

J

JACOB

Abraham's grandson, son of Isaac and Rebekah, born in the 18th century B.C. A shepherd. Jacob was also called Israel. He was seen as the father of the ancestors of the twelve tribes of Israel. All Israelites are therefore "sons of Jacob," "sons of Israel" or belong to "the house (family) of Israel."

JERUSALEM

The capital of Judea. An ancient royal city since the time of David. The world-wide religious center of Judaism with its Temple that was being rebuilt in Jesus' day. At each festival, particularly at Passover, crowds of pilgrims came to the capital. It was also the seat of religious and political Jewish authority. This is where the confrontation between Jesus and the leaders reached its climax and led to his condemnation and execution. At the end of the Jewish war, in 70 A.D., the town and the Temple were completely destroyed by the Roman army.

JOHN THE BAPTIST

Son of the priest Zechariah and Elizabeth, Mary's cousin. After a time in the desert, John called people to be converted and baptized on the banks of the Jordan. Jesus followed him for a while. Then Jesus took up where John the Baptist left off. John the Baptist only prepared Jesus' way; this is why he was called "the forerunner." John was executed by Herod Antipas.

JOHN

Name meaning "God spared." Apostle and evangelist. See page 21.

JORDAN

A river that runs along the eastern border of Palestine. Its source is situated at 900 feet above sea level. It flows into and out of Lake Tiberias. Then, in a deep valley with many twists and turns, it drops 1300 feet below sea level and opens into the Dead Sea. Despite many fords, it acts more as a frontier than a place of passage.

JOSEPH

A descendant of David. The husband of Mary, the mother of Jesus. The gospels speak of him during Jesus' youth. Not to be confused with Joseph, son of Jacob, who was sold into slavery by his brothers approximately seventeen centuries earlier.

JUDAS
A common name in Jesus' day. Judas Iscariot ("man of Cariot," from Judea) was one of the twelve apostles. He betrayed Jesus to the chief priests and received thirty coins in return. According to the gospels, Judas returned the money; he then committed suicide. This "blood money" was used to buy a field in which foreigners were buried, called "Field of Blood."

JUDEA
"Land of ravines." A mountainous region in southern Palestine having a warm, dry climate. Important cities include Jerusalem, the capital; Bethlehem, David's city; Hebron, where Abraham stayed; and Jericho, city of palm trees.

JUSTICE
Being fair means respecting the rights of others and observing God's law. God is fair. God judges all according to their innermost thoughts and their actions. God defends the poor person who is crushed by injustice. God calls everyone to justice and helps people to live according to the law of love.

K

KINGDOM
Israel had a wonderful memory of David's kingdom. But for a very long time no kings had emerged from this David's line. Many people hoped for a new David. Others hoped that God would come and establish the Kingdom. Jesus spoke a lot about God's Kingdom (the Kingdom of Heaven). This touched the people's deepest desire. But Jesus didn't define the Kingdom. He described it with images. It was like sowing seeds, like yeast. Jesus said that it had already come; at the same time, he said that it would come in the future.

L

LAKE TIBERIAS
This lake was also called the Sea of Galilee or the Lake of Gennesaret. It is 13 miles long and 6 miles wide and is 150 feet deep. The Jordan River flows through it. The lake is surrounded by hills. Jesus began his work on the shores of this lake and in fishing boats on it. This is where the gospels place the call of the apostles (Mark 1.12-20), many cures (Mark 1.21-34), the calming of the storm (Matthew 8.23-27), the multiplication of the bread (Mark 6.30-44) and the appearance of the resurrected Jesus (John 21.1-14).

LAMB
Traditionally, Hebrews were nomads. They raised sheep. On the night of their escape from Egypt each family slaughtered and ate a lamb — the Passover lamb, or the paschal lamb. Since then, Israelites have repeated the same tradition each year at Passover. They commemorate their liberation. For Christians, Jesus is the true paschal lamb because, through his death, all human beings have been liberated from sin and death.

LAYING ON HANDS
Placing hands on someone to bless, heal, give the Spirit, or give a mission or function in the Church.

LAW
This word signifies the commandments given by God through Moses to the people of Israel. It is also used to speak of the books in the Bible where

these commandments are found. In Jesus' day, many Jews had become slaves of this Law. They tried to live according to every detail forgetting to love God and their brothers and sisters. The gospels reject this point of view, which is not life-giving and which leads to death. The gospels proclaim the law of the Spirit and of love.

LEVITE
A member of the tribe of Levi. Levites worked for the Temple; some were musicians, singers or doorkeepers. They were not allowed in the Temple building or the entrance of the altar — places that were served by the priests.

LORD
This word is a royal title used to address the emperor (Acts 25.25). It is also a divine title used to address God. Jesus' disciples and the early Christians understood that Jesus was Lord or God. They refused to recognize the emperor as Lord and God.

LUKE
He wrote the third gospel and the Acts of the Apostles. See page 19.

M

MARK
Evangelist and Peter's companion in mission. See page 18.

MARY
Mother of Jesus. She is present throughout Jesus' whole life and at his crucifixion. See page 193.

MATTHEW
Also called Levi (Mark 2.13-17; Matthew 9.9-13). He is credited with writing the first gospel.

MESSIAH
See CHRIST.

MIRACLE
Marvelous event by which God's action is seen. The gospels tell of many of Jesus' miracles: exorcisms, healing the sick, actions in nature. Jesus refused to perform miracles to satisfy people's curiosity or to show off. His miracles were signs of God's love. Today many events that appear miraculous can be explained by science. But this should not stop us from searching for signs of God's love and action in nature, history and in our lives.

MOSES
Around the year 1250 B.C. (or perhaps much earlier in 1400

B.C.), Moses led the Israelite people, who were slaves in Egypt, through the desert to freedom. In God's name, Moses gave them the Law. Throughout history he continued to be known as the liberator and lawmaker for Israel. The gospels show Jesus speaking to Moses and Elijah during the Transfiguration (Mark 9.2-10). Jesus didn't come to abolish Moses' law but to fulfill it (Matthew 5.17).

MYRRH

Scented resin as perfume or an ointment. It was a very special gift; it was one of the gifts offered by the wise men to the infant Jesus.

N

NAZARETH

Village in Galilee where Jesus spent most of his life. See pages 7, 8, 9.

NERO

Roman emperor from 54 to 68 A.D. An emotionally unstable man, he both loved and killed those around him. He thought he was a great poet. He was accused of setting fire to Rome in 64 A.D. He turned the accusations against the early Christians and launched the first great persecution.

P

PARABLE

A colorful story with a hidden meaning. Jesus often spoke in parables. He used images as examples. He told stories. The sower sowed the seeds. The housewife mixed yeast with the dough. The son left his father and then returned. The Samaritan helped a wounded man. It was up to the listeners to find the hidden meaning – the seed is the word of God and the kind, generous Samaritan is our neighbor.

PASCHAL

Word meaning "related to Passover".

PASSOVER

The Jewish Passover is celebrated as the commemoration of the Israelites' flight from Egypt. Unleavened bread is eaten. A paschal lamb is sacrificed and eaten. Many pilgrims go to Jerusalem. Jesus was executed on the evening before Passover. For Christians this celebration takes on a new meaning. They don't forget the liberation of Israel. But they concentrate their celebration on Jesus' resurrection from the dead, a liberation that concerns all people.

PAUL

A Pharisee who became Christian. He was then the "Apostle to all Nations." See page 16.

PENTECOST

See pages 223 to 227.

PERSECUTION

Jesus was persecuted and put to death because the religious leaders were jealous and because the Roman rulers were cowardly. In the beginning, Romans saw Christians as a type of Jew; they considered Jesus' followers a dangerous sect. The religious leaders had Stephen stoned to death (Acts 7). Christians were persecuted for the first time under the emperor Nero (see NERO), and again under Domitian (81 to 96 A.D.) because they refused to recognize him as "Lord and God." When the gospels were written, Christians had already lived through several persecutions. They remembered what had happened to Jesus. They understood what it meant to "take up their cross and follow" him (Mark 8.34) or to be "treated badly for doing right" (Matthew 5.10).

PETER

His Hebrew name was Simon. He was a fisherman on the lake near

Galilee. Jesus called Simon and his brother, Andrew. He gave Simon the name of Peter which means "rock." As the leader of the Twelve, Peter followed Jesus enthusiastically. This, however, did not stop Peter from falling asleep on the night Jesus was arrested, nor from denying that he knew Jesus. Peter cried bitterly at his lack of courage. As a witness of the resurrection (Luke 24.34), he proclaimed the Good News. When he met Christians from the pagan tradition, he understood that it wasn't necessary for them to follow Jewish laws (Acts 10.1-48). He died as a martyr in Rome, in the year 64 or 67 A.D. Tradition has it that he was crucified upside down.

PHARISEE

These were zealous legal experts. They referred to themselves as being "separate." They were separated from the chief priests and from the common people, whom they despised. They had a lot of influence on townspeople and peasants, on merchants, craftspeople, and even on priests. They explained to them how to live the Law in everyday life. Jesus and the gospels were very critical of Pharisees. They are often seen as hypocrites and people who are only interested in the letter of the Law.

POOR

There were many poor people in Jesus' day. Who were they? Workers who earned a coin for a day's work when they could find work; peasants with huge debts, some of whom had to sell themselves as slaves; widows and orphans without any income; beggars; people out of work; the blind and the crippled. These people flocked to Jerusalem and to the gates of towns. They were often ridiculed. Everyone thought God didn't love them. But Jesus reached out to them. He spoke to them and asked them to follow him.

PRIESTS

Next to the high priests and the chief priests, they represented about ten percent of the country's population. They were in charge of ceremonies and sacrifices in the Temple. They received a tithe, an income tax that they were given directly. But often the tithe was not enough for them to live on, so they had to find other jobs.

PRODIGAL

Word meaning "wasteful." (See page 134.)

PROPHET

A prophet is someone who speaks in God's name, who reads meaning into the history of humanity. A prophet calls people to conversion. Israel had great prophets: Isaiah, Jeremiah, Ezekiel, Daniel. In Jesus' day the writings of these prophets were well known and often read in the synagogue. Many of the people who knew Jesus considered him to be a prophet. He didn't object to being called a prophet.

PSALM

Prayers and songs found, for the most part, in the book of the Bible called Psalms. They were used for prayer in the Temple, in synagogues and in families, and for personal prayer. They allow people to call out to God together, and serve as a reminder of the wonderful things God has done for the world. The Psalms are still sung and prayed today.

PURE/IMPURE
or CLEAN/UNCLEAN

In the Jewish religion a person had to be pure (clean) in order to meet God. This meant that one had to avoid eating certain foods, touching certain things, catching certain illnesses, or disobeying the Law. These things were thought to be contaminating, and people who were contaminated by them had to be "purified." There were different rituals of purification. Priests were given the responsibility of distinguishing between the pure (clean) and the impure (unclean). Having to pay so much attention to "purity" often made people slaves to meticulous cleanliness. Jesus reacted — what counted wasn't the exterior, but that the heart of the person was pure. It wasn't what entered the person that made one impure, but what evil acts came out of one's heart (Mark 7.14-23).

R

RABBI

A title of distinction used for a doctor of the Law. It can be translated as "Master!" or "My master."

RESURRECTION

Rising from the dead means going from death to life. In Jesus' day, many people believed that resurrection was possible. The gospels tell of Jesus bringing the dead back to life. But Jesus' resurrection is different. He didn't return to the life he had before his death. He went through death to new life.

REVEAL

Word meaning "lift the veil." God reveals the face of God, or is known. The Bible is the book of God's revelation. Thanks to the Bible, human beings can seek and discover God.

RICH

In Biblical times, wealth was seen as a blessing from God. In Jesus' day, rich people held the power in Palestine. Often the rich oppressed the poor. For centuries the prophets had denounced these injustices, "They smear the poor in the dirt" (Amos 2.7). Jesus said that it was difficult for a rich person to enter the God's Kingdom (Matthew 19.24).

RIGHTEOUS
See GOOD PEOPLE.

S

SABBATH
See page 66.

SADDUCEES

A group of lay people and priests who were rich, conservative and influential. Many of the chief priests belonged to this group. The Sadducees took advantage of the Roman presence. They collaborated with the Romans. They were opposed to new ideas. They didn't believe in resurrection from the dead. In many ways they were responsible for Jesus' execution.

SAMARITAN
See page 89.

SANHEDRIN
The Jewish High Council. There were 71 members: elders, high priests, scribes and doctors (= teachers) of the law. The Sanhedrin was under Rome's control. It took care of the internal government of the country and was responsible for justice. It met when Jesus was put on trial (Matthew 27.1).

SATAN
Word meaning "accuser," "adversary" and "enemy" of humanity and God. In the gospels, Satan represents what is bad, the forces of evil, the demon or the devil. He often battles with Jesus but is always defeated. (See DEMON.)

SAVIOR
Saving others means rescuing them from great danger, sickness, slavery, war, death, evil or sin. Throughout the Bible, God appears as the Savior. The disciples proclaim that Jesus is the Savior. Liberation comes through Jesus and not by observing the Law. "God's wonderful kindness is what saves you" (Ephesians 2.5).

SCRIBE
Expert in Jewish law. Doctor (= teacher) of the law. The scribes and the priests were those who led the people. Many scribes were Pharisees. Some were on the Sanhedrin. Jesus reproached them for being more interested in the Law than in the needs of the people.

SCRIPTURE
Writings. In the Christian Scriptures, "Scriptures" refer to the texts of the Hebrew Scriptures that existed in Jesus' day. The Hebrew Scriptures contained the history of the origins of the Jewish people, Moses' law, writings from prophets and wise people, and prayers such as the Psalms. These texts were read in all of the synagogues. They were seen as the people's tradition and the Word of God.

SHEPHERD
Shepherds watched flocks of sheep and goats. They led them to fields where they could graze and to water where they could drink.

Shepherds protected their flocks against wild animals and thieves. In the Bible, leaders are often compared to shepherds. Some are good, others evil. The gospels present Jesus as the good shepherd who knows his flock and sacrifices his life for it (John 10.11).

SICKNESS

In Jesus' day, sick people were thought to be punished by God or even possessed by a demon. Healing was seen as an act of God; healers were his intermediaries. The gospels show that Jesus refused to see sickness as punishment (John 9.1-3). They also show him healing the sick and chasing demons (Mark 5.1-20).

SINNER

A sinner is someone who, in God's eyes, does bad things. Sin is first of all found in the heart. The sinner is a slave to sin. Jesus came not to condemn sinners but to free them.

SON OF DAVID

Title given by the Jews to the Messiah whom they were expecting. They considered him to be a descendant (a son) of and a successor to David (a king). In the gospels, sick people and crowds referred to Jesus in this way (Matthew 20.30).

SON OF GOD

During his life on earth, Jesus spoke to God as his father, "Abba" (Mark 14.36). After Jesus' death and resurrection, the disciples understood much better that he was the "Son of God." He was much more than the Messiah whom everyone was expecting. God gave everything in giving his son, Jesus. The disciples understood that God could say to Jesus: "You are my own dear Son, and I am pleased with you" (Mark 1.11).

SON OF MAN

This expression can simply mean "the man" or "someone." But in Jesus' day, it also made people think of a vision that the prophet Daniel had that described the coming of the Son of Man at the end of time. He came on clouds in the sky to save the people during the judgement. When he spoke about himself, Jesus used the expression "Son of Man." Later, the early Christians understood that Jesus was the Son of Man who would come at the final judgement.

STAR

In ancient times, many people thought that stars were gods. In the Bible, stars are creatures of God. They witness to God's greatness. They are there to serve humanity. The image of the star is used to represent the twelve tribes of Israel and also the coming of the Messiah. A star guided the wise men from the East to the infant Jesus (Matthew 2.1-12).

SYNAGOGUE

Word meaning "gathering." It is most often used to refer to the building where the Jewish assembly met to pray and listen to the Word. There were synagogues in every town and village. The holy books were kept in a special place blocked off by curtains. A pulpit was used for public readings. Services were held mostly on the Sabbath and feast days. Jesus often went to the synagogue with his disciples.

T

TAX COLLECTORS

Employees of the Romans. They were in charge of collecting both income tax and also customs taxes. The amount of tax was set by the authorities. Often, tax collectors demanded more money and kept the difference for themselves. They were rich and despised by poeple. They were seen as sinners. Jesus spent time with them. Some, like Zacchaeus

(Luke 19.1-10) and Levi (Mark 2.13-17), were converted and decided to follow Jesus.

TEMPLE

The most important building in Jerusalem. The religious center for Judaism throughout the world. It existed from the time of King Solomon (10th century B.C.). It was destroyed and rebuilt. In Jesus' day, many renovations were under way. They were not finished until the year 64 A.D. The Temple was made of a large square surrounded by columns and a central building divided into three rooms: the entry way, the sanctuary and the Most Holy place (where the divine presence was located). The space around this building was divided into different zones. A place where everyone was permitted to go was the pagan's court. This area was separated from the rest by a wall that no non-Jew could cross under penalty of death. On the other side of the wall were the women's court, the men's court and the priests' court, where the sacrificial altar was located. Jesus went to the Temple many times, and he foretold of its destruction. The Temple was destroyed at the end of the Jewish war in the year 70 A.D., six years after its construction was completed.

TIME

See HOUR.

TWELVE

A number that is found frequently in the Bible, meaning wholeness. The twelve tribes of Israel represented all of Israel. Jesus chose twelve apostles. They were the leaders of the new Israel. The gospels called them the "Twelve." When Judas committed suicide, he was replaced by Matthias so that there would still be twelve apostles (Acts 1.12-26). In a vision of the future, Jesus spoke of the "twelve thrones to judge the twelve tribes of Israel" (Matthew 19.28).

W

WATER

Water is necessary for life. Without water the earth would produce neither fruit nor vegetables. Water is used for washing or cleaning. In Jesus' day and when the gospels were written, water was used for purification and baptism. It was the sign of God's life in men and women "like a flowing fountain that gives eternal life" (John 4.14).

WHITE

The color white represents innocence, joy, the glory of heaven and God's light. In the gospels, God's messengers were dressed in white (Mark 9.3, Acts 1.10). The early Christians wore white at baptism. This meant that they were purified and that they lived with Jesus Christ (Revelation 3.18).

WISE MEN

The name given to the foreigners who came to adore Jesus as an infant (Matthew 2.1-12). It could mean astrologers from Babylon, Arabia or Persia. The Bible says nothing of their number, the color of their skin, their names, nor whether they were kings.

WOMEN

In Jesus' day women played a secondary role in society. Jesus healed women (Luke 13.10-17). He spoke with the Samaritan woman (John 4.1-42). He stayed at Martha and Mary's house (Luke 10.38-42). Women followed him throughout Palestine (Luke 8.1-3) and as far as the cross (Matthew 27.55, 56). After the resurrection the women joined in prayer with the other followers of Jesus (Acts 1.14). They helped to elect Matthias (Acts 1.15-26), and received the power and gifts of the Holy Spirit at Pentecost (Acts 2.1-4, 18).

WORD OF GOD

The God of the Bible is a God who communicates with human beings. God speaks in thousands of ways. One of the most important ways is through Jesus, God's living Word (John 1.1). Both the Hebrew and Christian Scriptures show us how men and women discovered, understood and welcomed this Word. It is like a seed that falls on different types of earth (Mark 4.8-20).

Y

YEAR OF CELEBRATION

This expression refers to a Year of Jubilee or grace. According to Jewish law, every fifty years was special. It came after one week of years: 7 x 7 years = 49 + 1. On this occasion it was important to let the earth rest, to free slaves, to forgive debts and allow everyone to recover lost property. In Nazareth, Jesus declared that the Year of Jubilee had arrived (Luke 4.19). Some rejoiced, especially the poor. They had nothing to lose and everything to gain. Others were angry, especially the rich. They had a lot to lose.

Z

ZEALOT

Jewish revolutionaries who wanted to expel the Romans with armed battle and reestablish David's former kingdom. Barabbas, the prisoner who was freed during Jesus' trial, as well as the two men who were crucified with Jesus, may have been zealots. These revolutionaries played an important role in the Jewish war against Rome from 66 to 70 A.D. The war ended in Jewish defeat and resulted in the destruction of the holy city and the Temple. The apostle Jude Thaddeus was a member of this group before he became a disciple.

Table
of Contents

THE ROMAN EMPIRE
IN GOSPEL TIMES

BRETONS

GAULS

GERM

SPAIN

Rome

ITALY

NUMIDIANS

PERSIAN
GULF